MW00682137

Being Mentored

Getting What You Need

Vicki Garavuso

 **Higher Education**

Boston   Burr Ridge, IL   Dubuque, IA   New York   San Francisco   St. Louis
Bangkok   Bogotá   Caracas   Kuala Lumpur   Lisbon   London   Madrid   Mexico City
Milan   Montreal   New Delhi   Santiago   Seoul   Singapore   Sydney   Taipei   Toronto

Higher Education

BEING MENTORED: GETTING WHAT YOU NEED
Published by McGraw-Hill, a business unit of The McGraw-Hill Companies, Inc., 1221 Avenue of the
Americas, New York, NY, 10020. Copyright © 2010 by The McGraw-Hill Companies, Inc. All rights
reserved. No part of this publication may be reproduced or distributed in any form or by any means, or
stored in a database or retrieval system, without the prior written consent of The McGraw-Hill Companies,
Inc., including, but not limited to, in any network or other electronic storage or transmission, or broadcast
for distance learning.

Some ancillaries, including electronic and print components, may not be available to customers outside
the United States.

This book is printed on acid-free paper.
1 2 3 4 5 6 7 8 9 0 FGR/FGR 0 9

ISBN: 978-0-07-337835-0
MHID: 0-07-337835-6

Editor in Chief: *Michael Ryan*
Publisher: *David Patterson*
Sponsoring Editor: *Allison McNamara*
Marketing Manager: *James Headley*
Developmental Editor: *Jill Eccher, VanBrien & Associates*
Project Manager: *Meghan Durko*
Design Manager: *Allister Fein*
Designer: *Mary-Presley Adams*
Production Supervisor: *Louis Swaim*
Composition: *10/12 Times New Roman by Laserwords*
Printing: *45# New Era Matte by Quebecor Fairfield*

Library of Congress Cataloging-in-Publication Data

Garavuso, Vicki.
    Being mentored: getting what you need/Vicki Garavuso. —1st ed.
        p. cm.
    Includes bibiographical references.
    ISBN-13: 978-0-07-337835-0
    ISBN-10: 0-07-337835-6
    1. Mentoring in education. 2. Teachers—Training of. I. Title.
    LB1731.4.G37 2008
    371.102—dc22

                                                    2008042829

The Internet addresses listed in the text were accurate at the time of publication. The inclusion of a website
does not indicate an endorsement by the authors of McGraw-Hill, and McGraw-Hill does not guarantee the
accuracy of the information presented at these sites.

About *The Practical Guide Series*

New teachers face a seemingly endless set of challenges—classroom management, assessment, motivation, content knowledge, cultural responsiveness, inclusion, technology—just to name a few. Preparing for the profession can at times seem overwhelming. Teacher candidates may begin to see solutions to some of the anticipated challenges as they progress through a program of study but know that there are many that await them in their first classroom. Support by mentors and colleagues is crucial for beginning teachers, and this series is designed to bolster that guidance. *The Practical Guide Series* provides another level of support for these new and future professionals.

The series was conceived in response to concerns about teacher retention, especially among teachers in their first to fourth years in the classroom when mentorship and guidance play a crucial role. These titles offer future and beginning teachers a collection of practical advice that they can refer to in student teaching and in the early teaching years. Instructors of pre-service teachers can use these books to reinforce concepts in their texts with additional applications, use them to foster discussion, and help guide pre-service students in their practice teaching.

Besides addressing issues of basic concern to new teachers, we anticipate generating a level of excitement—one that a traditional textbook is hard-pressed to engender—that will further motivate entrants into this most essential profession with a contagious enthusiasm. A positive start to a teaching career is the best path to becoming a master teacher!

Alfred S. Posamentier, *Series Editor*
Dean, The School of Education,
The City College of New York

In memory of
Leslie Rowel Williams
A woman who always asked the best questions.

To
Jim, Vivianna, and Peri
For your constant love and support
I have a life made full with you.

Contents

Preface

When I thought about writing this book, the title, *Being Mentored: Getting What You Need,* came to me in a flash. I knew I wanted to write for the undergraduate student. I knew I wanted to talk about early childhood education and all of the wonderful approaches we use that I think should be influencing all levels of education, rather than early childhood educators constantly having to protect young children from inappropriate ideas and practices that are constantly being "pushed down" and assuming that children are students before they are children. Early childhood educators understand that caring and nurturance are the foundations of what we do. We work in holistic environments and consider the ecological development of the child, the family, the classroom, and the larger community. We know that children learn best by doing and exploring. We know that studying one topic can easily lead to another, and yet another still. We know that different children will learn differently. We know that being bilingual is an asset, not a deficit. We know that multiculturalism and multicultural curriculum happen as we include everyone in the life of the group. We know too that we are leaders in our own classrooms, but that the best leaders guide others to lead too. We know that our role is to empower children and so we help by giving them the tools—real and imaginary—to be lifelong learners. We try to ask good questions and make sure there will be enough time and ample space for exploration, discovery, and reinvestigation.

As an early childhood educator and as a teacher educator, I knew I also wanted to empower adults to take control of their own learning. I believe that, just as adults must understand how children learn, we should also know about how adults learn. If we can use these understandings to support our endeavors as lifelong learners, then our work will become even more meaningful, profound, and powerful.

I believe that in order to become a teacher of students at any age, you must not only be knowledgeable about content, you must be knowledgeable about *who* you will teach. For young children, teachers must know about child development, family and community cultures, and appropriate classroom pedagogy. The same can be said for instructors in adult classrooms, except that adults can understand the value of their experience and the knowledge they bring and share in these settings. College instructors, like teachers, should know more than the course content. They should know about the learning styles of their students, whether they be traditional-age undergraduates or the "new" adult undergraduate. College instructors must learn from the lived lives and narratives of their students. By thinking about this from an educator's perspective and putting it all together, we should get appropriate classroom pedagogy. And, from this paradigm, I believe that adults who are aware of what they bring to classrooms can use that awareness as a stepping-off place to create understandings of how they learn, what they want to learn, and how to get what they need in order to learn it.

As I began to write this book, someone said that undergraduates will not want to read something that had references to research or theories about adult learning and critical theory. Since this has not been the case in my own teaching experience, I strongly disagree. I believe that undergraduates need to be introduced to research and theory. Hopefully, this book will serve you beyond the mentoring literature. I hope that the works cited in this text will lead you to read more about adult education, educational philosophies, critical theory, social justice education, and policies that affect young children, their families, and early childhood educators in different settings. I know that in doing this work, I was educated as well. Finding and examining these resources and citations opened doors to new knowledge that I know will influence my work in the future.

Throughout my own teaching career, I have been fortunate to receive quality mentoring. One important mentoring experience occurred when I decided to attend graduate school to become a teacher. I was working on my first master's degree and, as part of a new teacher cohort, was assigned an advisor. Her role was to supervise new teachers in the field, to meet with us individually, and to mentor the group at weekly meetings. She failed miserably on all counts. She missed appointments for observations and reflections and seemed distracted at group meetings. And, although our cohort was made up of mostly early childhood majors, she knew little about how practices in preschools differed from elementary education.

Luckily, the college responded to the group's concerns, and the head of the initial certification program stepped in to support us. I met with her often, and she was truly interested in my questions and viewpoints. We spoke about what it was like to be the first in your family to go to college, having this in common. She helped me find a path through graduate school, checking on me when the advisement group disbanded. She followed me into my first classroom. Her practical advice helped me with the challenges I faced as a novice teacher, especially my relationships with parents and my assistant teacher. And, many years later, she took me out to lunch to help me understand why I didn't get that first college appointment I had so desperately wanted.

My first teaching job was in a small nursery school where the director, a seasoned kindergarten teacher, and I were hired the same year. Fortunately, when the three of us came together we found that we all firmly believed in a child- and family-centered approach to working with young children.

As a new teaching staff we spent a great deal of time talking about children and families. We discussed our work often and, as a new teacher, I felt supported in my efforts to uncover and share what I discovered about teaching and learning. It was the 1980s and together we learned about autism, ADD, and AIDS. We sought out experts who came and spoke to us and to the parents about the importance of the work we did. We worked closely with support agencies to meet children's and families' diverse needs. We went on book-buying staff outings, bringing back literature that represented the international population of this school. We shared our observations and insights about the children in our classrooms and helped each other develop parent orientations, family conferences, and appropriate experiences and curriculum. In a sense, we mentored each other.

Ten years later, when I decided to return to graduate school, wanting to move up the career ladder, my director became an even more powerful mentor. She created opportunities for me to develop and apply my personal vision as a leader. I ran workshops at the nursery, supervised a novice teacher, and helped plan an expansion of the program—including input into its architectural design. I wrote my master's thesis on the history and development of the center. And, as a result of being in a mentoring environment, I grew as a teacher and took with me a deep professional respect and lasting affection for the staff and families who helped me learn firsthand about early childhood education.

At this time yet another mentor stepped into my life. She was a master teacher, an exquisite writer, a brilliant mind, and a generous spirit. I had met her at a national early childhood conference. As the audience broke into small working groups, I found myself with her. Her name was vaguely familiar to me—I recognized her as an important figure in early childhood teacher education. I don't remember what the workshop was about, but I do remember asking her what I should do with the rest of my life. This was the time when I was contemplating leaving the classroom for administration. She answered, as any good teacher would, by turning the question back to me. Then, she asked what I was already doing with my life, and told me to focus on the things I liked most. Looking back, I recall how this brief interaction led me to uncover how much I enjoyed working with other teachers as we reflected on our practices in early childhood settings.

Years later, as a doctoral student, I met her again and she became my mentor. After a few months of meeting regularly, I mentioned our first encounter. She naturally had no recollection of it, but to me it was a welcomed coincidence. Interestingly, she had just received a grant to study the effects of mentoring on doctoral students. Under her tutelage, I joined a cohort of other doctoral students who also participated in mentored relationships. Students and professors came together in a weekly seminar to discuss our research and share our writing. It was, without doubt, one of the most demanding and intimidating times in my academic life. This brilliant woman always asked the best questions, often with a philosophical bent that made me think beyond my most obvious answers. It was hard work, yet I came away knowing I had something worth sharing with experienced educators and new teachers alike.

I wrote *Being Mentored: Getting What You Need* to help you, the teacher education candidate, be in a position to have similar high-quality mentoring experiences. In this book, I will help you understand how mentoring relationships work, both from the perspective of the mentor and of the student, and how you can derive maximum benefit from them. I will discuss different approaches mentors take and how to work with specific kinds of mentors, including professors, fieldwork supervisors, and experienced classroom teachers. I will show you how to address typical challenges that may arise. Effective communication is the key to a good mentoring relationship, and I will show you, in detail, how to establish and maintain good communication.

I have subtitled this book "a pragmatic guide" because I believe so strongly that what we know comes from experience. It is in the everyday experiences of feeling and reflecting that we come to know what it is to be a student and to be a teacher. It is also from these everyday experiences that we take what we need to develop, share with others, add to future experiences, and have an effect on our world.

In Chapter 1, I lay the groundwork for understanding why having a mentoring relationship will support your learning. I look at different theories about how adults learn, again believing that having this understanding can empower you, the adult learner. In defining the different theories about how adults learn, I parallel early childhood practices and use a constructivist approach, attempting to help you feel more comfortable with the idea that learning at any age takes time and repetition.

In Chapter 2, I begin with a practice dear to the hearts of early childhood professionals, a humanistic approach to education, and apply it to mentoring. I assume that this is where we all should begin, whether we are being with children or being mentored. From this safe place, children and adult learners come to know that learning itself is the life of the classroom. Within a humanistic setting, you, the learner, are encouraged to think without limits about what you are learning. In doing so, you are empowered to be reflective and to think consciously about your work—to name it and discuss it with others. Using this concept, teachers learn to become reflective in their own practices and name what they do. In this same way, adults need to become reflective in a broader context. This includes critical reflection and naming issues around the child care/education setting in which you work, your own earlier education, and your current experiences in college.

In Chapter 3, I offer ideas about how to approach someone whom you might like to have as a mentor and what to look for in a good mentor. I look at the literature on mentoring and the many definitions of the mentor and the protégé. Naturally, finding someone who can become your mentor will at times be a matter of finding someone likeable and knowledgeable. Yet, there are times when you as a protégé may be placed in a mentoring relationship and have no choice. I talk about what mentors read when they want to learn about mentoring, and I use those writings to help you understand how to develop a relationship with a mentor and get what you need from that relationship.

In Chapter 4, I discuss specific types of mentors you may encounter. I talk about relationships with different mentors in different places including your undergraduate experiences in an early childhood teacher education program, specifically examining clinical supervision. I also examine the mentoring literature pertaining to formal and informal mentoring relationships, including on the job and social supports.

In Chapter 5, I return to adult learning styles. Again, if you are to take ownership of your own learning, then you must become cognizant of the ways you learn best. By naming these learning styles, you can contextualize expectations that you and your mentor may have of the mentoring relationship, and in identifying these expectations, you can take into account which motivating factors will help you achieve what you will come to define as a "successful" mentoring relationship. In this section, I also consider the literature's advice on "making the match" and its implications for a successful mentoring relationship. And, if the choice of mentor is not someone with whom you identify, I explore some of the literature that addresses race and ethnicity, gender, and age differences and how these should be negotiated within a mentoring relationship.

In the final chapter, I discuss how having had a mentoring relationship can be used as a resource should opportunities arise to mentor others. In mentoring others, especially in early childhood education settings, the "new mentor" should not only help those who follow in teacher education programs, but also in a broader sense, help those who otherwise would remain silent. This notion of mentoring is another facet of integrated and contextualized learning and teaching that, most importantly, addresses what it means to mentor for equity and social justice in early childhood care/education settings as well as in the broader early childhood profession.

And finally, I call on those in the field of early childhood education, from classroom teachers to teacher educators to policy makers, to examine the inequities that our profession has struggled to make right. Choosing to become a teacher of young children is related to much more than how one feels about being with children. It is a choice you should make with the realization that much work needs to be done to afford young children safe, nurturing, challenging, and rewarding environments. It should also be a choice made with the understanding that early childhood educators must challenge notions that what we do is "just glorified baby-sitting," or that teaching young children is "just watered-down, first grade stuff." It is a choice to be made with the knowledge that we actually have much to offer that educators at all levels could use.

Ours is a profession that struggles to hold onto our beliefs and practices. It is a profession that must support our own by talking about our aspirations for children and ourselves, our actual daily work in classrooms and child care centers, and our struggles for recognition as professionals with pay parity in the field of education. Therefore, as you develop more sophisticated practices and achieve greater influence in your career as a teacher, this book will show you why it is important to support those who follow by becoming a mentor to others.

Being Mentored is aimed at demystifying the college setting as well as student teaching experiences. Most of all, *Being Mentored: Getting What You Need* will show you how to develop a mentoring relationship with someone who can listen, who can lend emotional support when you need it, and who can foster and scaffold your learning and guide you to your own questions, explorations, and understandings.

I would also like to say at the outset that I am fully aware that mentoring relationships are seldom as intense or profound as this work suggests. I would hope that you and your mentor can glean from these pages the formats and particular recommendations that will work for you both. While this book is focused on mentoring relationships, including some that are mandatory to undergraduate teacher education, my notion of a mentor is not restricted to a formal definition. Sometimes you may need to connect with a classmate or peer who is more experienced. Sometimes you may need to develop support from friends and family. And as the literature on mentoring shows, a single definition of mentoring does not exist, not by mentors themselves or by people who study mentoring (Mullen, Cox, Boettcher, and Adoue 2000).

More than the "perfect" mentoring relationship, I would hope that you use these ideas to develop connections to those people you have identified in your college, in your work site, or in your community who will share their knowledge and help you navigate through your professional teaching career.

Finally, one of the things I set out to do in this book was to empower the undergraduate student, in this case the often marginalized early childhood education student and the child care provider and teacher, by writing a book that would not only be about mentoring but would encompass other issues faced by traditional and "new" undergraduates. Hopefully, you will use this work as a source of strength when confronting these issues as you navigate the undergraduate experience and to name and offer others the knowledge and strengths you bring into adult classrooms, in settings with children, and as a future mentor. I hope that you will use the methods and ideas offered in *Being Mentored: Getting What You Need* to locate, develop, grow within, and mature from a productive mentoring relationship.

Most importantly, I hope that this book will help you come away with skills to not only assess what someone else in the college setting can do for you, but what you can do for yourself, and that in your search for a compassionate, knowledgeable, empowering, pragmatic, mentor as change-agent, you will not overlook the importance that your own experiences, talents, intellect, and vision bring to the relationship.

Mentoring, Transformative Learning, and the Teacher Education Candidate

An introduction to mentoring, focusing on how mentors are integral to becoming a good teacher

❖ The Value of Being Mentored, Particularly for Teacher Candidates
❖ Diverse Undergraduates, Diverse Learners
❖ Initiative, Experience, and Transformative Learning
❖ Mentoring as an Integral Part of Learning to Become a Teacher

The Value of Being Mentored, Particularly for Teacher Candidates

Teaching, perhaps more than any other profession, is a skill that is learned through modeling and emulation. By observing master teachers in the classroom, learning from them, and applying what you learn, you will discover how to become an accomplished teacher. For this reason, most teacher education programs around the country require fieldwork and supervised student teaching before you can be licensed. In fact, in most programs, you will be assigned a mentor or supervisor to guide you through this process. Being mentored, therefore, is not a choice but a necessity—an integral part of preparing to become a teacher.

Throughout the cultures of the world, there are many examples of mentors: the guru, the rabbi, the lama, the shaman, and the imam. In each case, a teacher or advisor guides a less experienced person. The word *mentor* comes from Homer's *Odyssey,* where Odysseus, away from home on his epic journey, entrusts the care of his son Telemachus to his loyal friend Mentor. At one point, when Telemachus goes off to search for his father, the god Athena disguises herself as Mentor and guides Telemachus. Yet, even though Athena is a god and has the ability to see the future—that Odysseus will return unharmed—she assigns Telemachus tasks that he must accomplish so that he will mature into a leader in his own right. While different disciplines stress different features of mentoring, in most definitions, the mentor is often someone older, wiser, and as in the case of Athena, someone who can more clearly see the purpose and envision the outcome. The mentor, therefore, is someone who should insist that you experience for yourself the steps required to realize your vision.

State education departments across the nation have rewritten teacher certification requirements to include fieldwork as a prerequisite before student teaching placements can be offered to the candidate. Fieldwork recognizes the foundation of good teacher education: theory (course work and readings) must be supported and exemplified by practice (through observations and/or participation in what actually happens in real classroom settings). Fieldwork does not always include working directly with children, but may instead involve recording what goes on in classrooms as you observe children and teachers. For the traditional undergraduate student, who attends college full-time and is not otherwise employed, fieldwork is often integrated into a larger schedule of classes and course work. But for the "new" undergraduate, who is likely to be employed full-time and attend school part-time, fulfilling field assignments becomes much more difficult. Given these challenges, getting the most from your mentoring relationships becomes crucial.

Your mentors, whether they are your professors, supervisors at your fieldwork and internship sites, or experienced teachers in the classroom, can help you identify and navigate the challenges you may confront.

A satisfying and productive mentoring relationship can deepen your knowledge and strengthen your skills. It can help you succeed in college by providing many opportunities for you to take responsibility for your own learning. For many teacher candidates, the mentoring relationship can be a transforming experience. But, like any relationship, it must be initiated, developed, and nurtured. Particular rules apply, and particular obstacles and pitfalls have to be navigated or avoided. In order to make the most of your undergraduate college experience, and your preparation as a teacher of young children in particular, you will need to become skilled at how to manage these challenges, learn from these experiences, define your goals, and evaluate your growth. In managing these challenges, you can get what you need from your teacher education.

Box 1-1

Mentors can help you answer the following common questions:

- How will I schedule the time to fulfill mandated fieldwork and student teaching assignments?
- If I work full-time while attending college, how can I find a site to visit before, during, or after work hours? Are there weekend programs or twenty-four child care centers that I can use to fulfill my requirements?
- If I am already working in an educational setting, can I use that site for field assignments? Do I want to? Why or why not?
- How will I know if I am observing quality teaching? And what if I am not?
- How can my professor/supervisor/mentor help me with this problem?

Ramon

Ramon, a recent graduate of early childhood education, had kept up our mentoring relationship. He had taken a job in a day care center in Brooklyn, teaching four-year-olds. He asked that I come to see him in his new classroom. The class included children that were registered with the Department of Education for universal prekindergarten, children who were registered only for day care, and children who were registered for both. I visited Ramon in early October after the children had left for the day. We spoke about the children and families that made up this community. Ramon said he was excited to be working in this center and was anxious to have a positive impact on these children's early school experiences. He spoke passionately about his belief in giving children choices stating, "There are so many times they don't get to choose, and people are always telling them what to do. I think if they're going to make good decisions later in life they have to make choices all the way through, even starting now."

As I have often done with new teachers, I suggested we look at each area of the room and talk about how the children were using it so far. As a first year teacher, he worked hard to get everything just right. At the door, he had hung a "Who is here today?" chart using children's pictures along with their names; he set up a graph for children to indicate their work choices; he had a picture-based job chart and a daily schedule that could be changed according to the special events for each day. He placed all of these charts and graphs where children could touch them, use them, and read them.

Ramon and I looked at the block area and he mentioned that he remembered our class discussion about not placing all the same blocks together since it would make for better traffic flow, usage, and cleanup. He said the children were just beginning to use the area and that he would add vehicles and furniture after they became more familiar and comfortable with actually building with the blocks. He said he hoped to make blocks a larger area if he could negotiate with his director to allow him to remove the large plastic table and frame that housed the nonfunctioning computer.

We also spoke about how the children were using the dress-up area. Ramon had inherited large bins full of plastic utensils, plates, and pretend food. He was concerned about the "big mess all the time" and that "the kids just dump everything into the pretend fridge without really thinking about it." I asked him what he wanted the children to get from these materials, and he said, "Well, I know that playing house is really important to this age. I want them to feel that they can use whatever they need to, but it's always too messy and they kick things on the floor and just dump things anywhere during cleanup." I asked if he had a specific number of children allowed in each area, and he quickly responded, "Yes, usually four children in an area." "Well," I replied, "why do you have twelve plates, and seven forks, and nine cups? Besides orderliness what about trying to do some math at the same time?" Ramon thought a moment and said, "Oh, you mean if there are four kids, then they could do one-to-one correspondence with four plates, four forks, and four cups?" I added, "And, when things are matching colors, they could do other kinds of sorting, and cleanup will be easier too." Ramon smiled and said, "That's why I asked you to come visit me. I knew you'd help me see these things and figure some of this out."

During the intervening weeks, Ramon and I only spoke briefly. When I was finally able to meet with him, sometime in January, Ramon told me about what had happened when the universal prekindergarten staff developer from the Department of Education came to see his room. He laughed and said that although she complimented him on how neat and well-organized his room was, she looked at the dress-up area and asked why there were so few pretend food items. She suggested he order more so children could have a larger selection. She also asked why same-shape blocks were sorted on more than one shelf, saying that she thought all the same shapes should go together. Ramon said that she also told him that he needed to put up a schedule showing the times of day that each activity took place and that it should be big enough for any adult visiting the room to be able to read it easily.

He continued with his story, again starting to laugh as he told it. A month or so after this visit, the day care was undergoing review for recertification. The consultant responsible for public day care settings in the borough came to visit. She also complimented Ramon on his classroom. She suggested that the schedule that he put up didn't need to be so large and should be posted outside the room so parents could see it, and that he be sure the menus for breakfast and lunch be posted alongside.

Ramon told me that he had decided not to destroy the larger schedule, but would make a second one and post it outside. He said he understood how important it was for parents to know what their children did all day and what they had to eat. Since he knew that the larger schedule was totally ignored by the children and was taking up valuable wall space, he decided to take it down and put it in the closet, hanging it up only when he knew the Department of Education staff developer would come back to his room.

Luckily for Ramon, he had not only been mentored by a college professor, but his student teaching placement was with a master prekindergarten teacher who had helped him develop a strong sense of himself as a professional educator of young children. Ramon is able to think about the everyday impacts that his decisions have on the children he teaches. He has been able to return to his previous mentors and ask them for input when he feels overwhelmed or unsure of his choices.

Ramon has been a head teacher for two years now. He has won districtwide recognition for his teaching. He has also facilitated in the development of a parent support group that serves the many recent immigrant families in the center. And, as Ramon has said, "I like working in groups. I wish I could find other ways to keep up the kinds of conversations we had in class. I think one of the things I'm going to do is try to get the other pre-K teachers at this school to meet, like they did at my student teaching placement. Even though we sometimes have professional development workshops, I think we should be meeting more to talk about what's going on in our classrooms, and about specific children . . . help each other figure out what we can do better or what certain children need." In one of our last visits together, Ramon spoke about how he uses some of the ways that he was supervised in his conversations with other teachers, especially asking questions and listening carefully to the answers. And most importantly, Ramon described how he has redefined his relationship with the Department of Education consultant, helping her understand why he does what he does in his classroom.

- Have you ever had an experience when more than one person expects you to follow different instructions regarding the same issue? How did you negotiate this?
- Think about a time when you may have felt powerless. What did it feel like? Did you do anything to address this? What? Was it resolved to your satisfaction? How did you feel at the conclusion?
- Think about a particular support system that might help you resolve this kind of issue. How would the answers of your coworkers, your director or principal, or your mentor or supervisor differ? What might you learn from each perspective?

Diverse Undergraduates, Diverse Learners

While many of you have become knowledgeable about how children learn, you will also want to become knowledgeable about your own learning processes in order to have a productive relationship with a mentor. Understanding theories about lifelong learning can help you situate and reflect on your motivation, communication style, assumptions, and interpretations. The more you understand about how you learn, the better you can communicate and build trust with your mentor, undertaking the processes of making and sharing meaning together with your own personal growth as the goal.

The Traditional Undergraduate

If you are a traditional undergraduate, that is, a young adult who has come to college directly from high school, you come to college with recent school experience. You are probably up on the latest technologies, have few time constraints, and are secure in your role as a student. Often you have to deal with your parents' expectations of your performance in college, and you are dealing with the stresses of forming social relationships. Therefore, as a young adult, you may be more likely to focus on and be motivated by others' approval and rewards (Werring 1987). Interestingly, the more you are involved in the social life of the college, the greater your learning and personal development will be. According to Graham and Donaldson (1999), as a traditional-aged college student, you may benefit most through student-student interactions because these have direct positive impacts as you learn habits, values, and knowledge from your peers.

According to a study conducted in 1997 by Eppler and Harju, most traditional students approach their education with either a *performance orientation* (external motivation such as grades) or a *learning orientation* (optimism and inner motivation). Those students who come to college thinking that performance is most important also believe that the greater the effort one makes to learn something, the lower the ability you have in that area. For example, a student who is struggling with biology must not have much ability in science. Unfortunately, students with a performance orientation may stop trying to achieve their goals because they feel that their efforts are in vain.

Eppler and Harju believe that moving from a performance orientation to a learning orientation can be done through individual efforts or through counseling. Those students with a learning orientation are often older and have spent more years in college; therefore, Eppler and Harju believe that the actual college experience itself contributes to the traditional students' ability to transform their orientations. Hopefully having a mentoring experience will also support this paradigm shift.

As a more traditional undergraduate, you may begin a mentored relationship in much the same way that you begin your relationship to learning in the college setting. William Perry, who was a professor at Harvard University, studied how the experiences of traditional undergraduate students influenced their dispositions toward learning itself. According to Perry (1999), as a traditional student you will advance through specific stages in the way you think about learning that often parallel your relationship to your teachers. If you are someone who began your higher education with a set viewpoint regarding issues of truth and morality, experiences interactions through an us-vs.-them lens, and values obedience to authority above all, hopefully by the end of your undergraduate career, you should have moved to what Perry calls "the evolving of commitments" (1999, 65). While there are many intervening stages, Perry claims that at this culminating stage you should feel a sense of urgency to make meaning in your life, responding to unresolved issues from your past or current experiences. Because you experience a developed sense of trust and an ability to examine issues or ideas from differing perspectives that allow critical thinking, you should also discover that you are committed to attempting new endeavors.

The "New" Undergraduate

You are a "new" undergraduate, or nontraditional college student, if you are someone over twenty-four years old. As a new undergraduate, you are more likely to have been out of school for a while, often returning by way of a community college, attending part-time, and commuting to classes. Often new undergraduates are heads of households whose outside school responsibilities include full-time employment, child care, elder parent care, and community-based commitments. You are often motivated by career choices and requisite degrees for advancement. You spend less time on campus, and participate less in the social aspects of college life. You may be the first in your family to attend an institution of higher education and, interestingly, often cite being a positive role model for your own children as one of the reasons you decided to attend college. Although you may be doubtful about your academic abilities, you bring life experiences that are often qualitatively different than the "traditional" undergraduate who comes to college directly from high school.

Many new undergraduates in early childhood education have had experience in classroom settings as assistant teachers or paraprofessionals. Others have been lead teachers, but now must earn bachelor's degrees for licensure because certification requirements have changed. And still others are interested in starting a new career and consider teaching to be the best use of their skills. Within "the hidden curriculum of adult life" (Kegan 2000, 45) these skills include being a parent, earning a living, caring for others, and attending to increasingly challenging social and technological aspects of daily life.

The nontraditional student is often seen through the lens of adult education research. Studies that consider the experiences of the nontraditional student are relatively fewer, but then again, this may be because the new undergraduate is just that—newer to college and therefore a newer subject in the research about college attendees.

As an adult student, you most likely believe that learning is a goal unto itself. Using this orientation, you are motivated by the belief that your efforts actually enhance your abilities and will lead to your success (Eppler and Harju 1997). Since you bring a wealth of knowledge and experience to the college classroom, you look at learning through the lens of these life experiences and expect to apply what you already know to what you are actively learning. Setting up learning for learning's sake is related to higher achievement.

As a new undergraduate you are open to learning in cooperative groups and do not feel that the teacher holds and disseminates all knowledge. You do not see yourself as a passive learner and resist the idea that achievement is only measured by how much of that same information is retained and repeated.

As an adult learner, you use your life experiences as a resource and as a place from which you observe and analyze the outside world, in many instances adding valuable insights to what may have been considered "given facts." As Sawchuk (2003, cited in Foley 2005) describes the nontraditional student, often represented by the working-class adult, you are someone who brings rich cultural frameworks to your learning within the university. Foley (2005) goes on to identify an adult working-class learning style as "collective, mutual and solidaristic. People exchange knowledge . . . [using] each other's differences, which become group resources" (2005, 40). In all college classrooms, but especially in teacher education classrooms, these insights add to everyone's understandings of the communities and schools in which ethnic minority families and nontraditional educators often work or live.

The nontraditional college student of teacher education can also be considered the nontraditional classroom teacher. Latino, Asian, African American, and Native American children now represent over 36% of the student population, while only 14% of K–12 teachers are ethnic minorities (Recruiting New Teachers 2000, cited in Clark, Riojas, and Bustos 2002). While the need for ethnic minority teachers is advanced in the literature that makes a strong case for exposing all children to educators of all nationalities (Fox and Gay 1995; Jenks, Lee, and Kanpol 2001; Kappner and Lieberman 2002; Quiocho and Rios 2000; Rintell and Pierce 2003), there are many reasons why minorities are choosing professions other than teaching: new opportunities in fields historically closed to minorities and women, higher salaries and greater prestige, and opportunities for advancement and better working conditions. Still researchers point to the inequities in education across the grades that ethnic minorities in the United States experience. One of the most effective ways to address the gap between children's home and school experiences is to support and encourage those who know the community and cultures of the children they teach, allowing them to lead in classroom settings.

Whether you are a traditional or a new undergraduate, by being mentored you will come to recognize your strengths as a student and a teacher. And, in partnership with your mentor, you will learn to recognize and/or create opportunities for learning, how to refine your reflections on your own learning, and how to pull these skills together as you define your own success.

Initiative, Experience, and Transformative Learning

There are many theories (and some controversy about the validity of research) concerning the characteristics of adult learners. Becoming familiar with some of these theories can make available other important contexts for the mentoring relationship.

Malcolm Knowles (1990), a preeminent scholar in the field of adult education, has defined the adult learner as someone who is self-motivated and takes the initiative to find opportunities to learn in order to meet the needs of particular situations, not just to learn discrete subjects. For example, the impetus for teacher candidates to attend college is often new certification requirements.

Knowles also differentiates between the child and adult learner. He draws attention to the term *pedagogy,* which derives from the Greek *paid,* meaning "child," and *agogus,* meaning "leader of." Thus, pedagogy literally means the art and science of leading children. If we stay with the notion that the teacher or mentor is the leader of the child, then the child learner remains a dependent learner. Instead of pedagogy, I prefer the term *andragogy,* which refers to a learner who is not dependent on another for the information he or she seeks.

For Knowles, the andragogical model provides a way of looking at the needs of the adult learner through a different set of assumptions than we usually assign to young

Box 1-2

Knowles's andragogical model and how it meets the needs of the adult learner

- *The need to know.* Adults need to know why they need to learn something before they begin to learn it. They are motivated to learn things that will satisfy their needs and interests.
- *The learners' self-concept.* Adults have a notion of themselves as being responsible for their own decisions and therefore their own learning. An adult's orientation to learning is life-centered; therefore, the appropriate way to organize adult education is through the analysis of experience.
- *The role of the learners' experience.* Adults have greater and more varied experiences than do children or younger adults. They will display a wider range of individual differences than a group of younger people. These differences will lead to a wider variety of responses to educational techniques and situations. Adults have a deep need to be self-directing; therefore, the role of the teacher is to engage in a process of mutual inquiry with the adult learner, rather than to transmit his or her knowledge to the learner and then evaluate his or her conformity to it.
- *Readiness to learn.* Adults come ready to learn those things they need to address real-life situations and problems.
- *Orientation to learning.* Adults are life-centered in learning, as opposed to the subject-centered approach of younger people. The most effective adult learning takes place when the new information is applied to real-life contexts and situations.
- *Motivation.* The most effective motivator is the internal pressure to keep growing and developing, whether for job-related or personal reasons.

learners. He acknowledges that even adults need to begin with a didactic model when they know nothing about the subjects they're studying. But, unlike the child, as an adult you are then able to learn more about the subject through your own initiative (Knowles 1990).

Still, there have been many criticisms of the andragogical approach. Some argue that andragogy presents an image of adults as society expects them to be and not as they really are. Others add that both andragogy and pedagogy involve preconceived notions of how both adults and children learn. Andragogy is also criticized for ignoring the contexts of race, class, gender, language, sexual orientation, or ability. And, personal qualities such as autonomy and self-direction, that are often considered desirable in Western cultures, may contradict the values of other cultures. For example, many cultures value humility and commitment to the good of the group; the individual may be expected to defer to elders or accept group consensus. Therefore, it is important to acknowledge that culturally influenced dispositions and habits can also have a profound impact on the mentoring experience.

Many undergraduates come to university classrooms having experienced what Brazilian educational philosopher Paolo Freire (1970) would characterize as the "banking model" of schooling. These models emphasize the authority of the teacher, where he or she "deposits" information and skills into students. How *much* one knows rather than *how* one comes to know it, becomes important. Considering what we know about adult learners, the "banking approach" would be anathema to adults pursuing lifelong education. Rather, Freire calls for students and teachers to become partners in problem posing and investigation. He believes that it is in the act of discourse that teacher and student come to share understandings about each other's experiences and about concepts in relation to these experiences.

Therefore, optimal conditions for adult learners should include

- Opportunities to be actively involved in assessing, planning for, carrying out, and evaluating your own learning.
- Opportunities to be self-directing.
- Recognition that learning occurs best with internal motivation.
- A readiness to learn, which is linked to a specific need to know.
- Drawing upon life experience so that learning will have meaning.
- Using others' experience to enrich your own learning.
- Opportunities for the immediate application of what is being learned.
- Mentoring that develops and maintains a supportive climate promoting the conditions necessary for learning to take place.

With all this talk about experience, it would be helpful to have a definition and to look at how experiences influence learning and learning styles. Most students of early childhood education are familiar with the ideas of American philosopher and educator John Dewey. Dewey wrote extensively about one of the most fundamental notions concerning learners and learning, that is, our ability to learn in the midst of experiencing and from having had an experience. Another important concept relating to experience comes from Dewey's definitions of pragmatism. One of the main principles of pragmatist philosophy is that "theory comes out of experience and is accountable to it" (Seigfried 2002, 51). Dewey believed that theory and practice are interwoven. He wrote that there is no such thing as being separate from the world and that we are always participating in the world. And, because we are always participating in the world, we shape it. This practical way of knowing comes from inquiry and the shared experiences of a community of multiple voices. And, for Dewey, we seek to know not only for knowledge's sake, but because we wish to make changes that have an effect on the world.

For Dewey (1916/1958) experience is a combination of both active and passive components. During the active portion of an experience, one is *trying*, or experimenting. This is considered active because it involves your action upon some aspect of your environment and produces change. The passive element of experience occurs when one *undergoes* the experience. This means that once you have acted upon something, it changes and, in turn, you undergo the consequences of this change. For Dewey, the significance of having of an experience occurs when "the change made by action is reflected back into a change made in us . . ." (1916/1958, 163). Thinking and learning take place in how you consciously perceive the change and connect it to past experience.

As you do something, something is also done to you. You take an action, and you undergo the consequences of that action. You learn something by reflecting on the experience. As Dewey wrote, you don't learn from just having an experience, but from the analysis of experience. It is in the doing, being in, and reflecting upon the value of the relationship between the thing and the consequences of having acted on the thing, that add to your ability to make meaning of an experience.

For Dewey, the *value* of an experience comes from your perceptions of experiences and the connections you make between previous and new experiences. Therefore, as you think about adult learning and teacher education in particular, you can see how Dewey's insights are important to the mentoring relationship. Since learning to be a teacher is so richly connected with concrete experience, for example, when you observe or work with a master teacher in a classroom, what you learned about teaching in theory, to some extent, no longer applies. You learn not only by observing other teachers but also by reflecting on the experience of observing. You must make the transition from learning about teaching in the abstract to the actual experience of teaching, *and* by reflecting on the experience of teaching. In much the same way, you will not only learn by being mentored, but by being conscious of how to reflect on the mentoring relationship, making the most of that experience.

Dewey also wrote about a concept called "plasticity" (1916/1958). Plasticity is what allows us to hold on to what is important in an experience and make use of it in a later situation. Plasticity is also the ability to adapt to new environments without losing your own personal perspectives. For example, almost everyone modifies their actions and behaviors according to the situation they find themselves in, such as behaving one way with your friends and another way with your professors. These behaviors lead to the development of dispositions or, in other words, what you bring with you that influences how you approach and reflect on experiences.

Dewey also refers to the contradiction faced by learners who consider themselves "mature" and therefore have already accomplished their growth. Most adults would be outraged if anyone suggested they had no further possibilities for growth. But here's the catch: even though in our society we assign a negative connotation to immaturity, in fact, someone or something that is immature always has the potential for further growth. Therefore as an adult learner, a disposition that embraces your own immaturity in particular areas also allows you to recognize your potential in those areas.

Finally, according to Dewey, dependence is also an asset. While dependence, like immaturity, might have a negative connotation, Dewey puts it this way, "The positive and constructive aspect of possibility gives the key to understanding the two chief traits of immaturity: dependence and plasticity" (1916/1958, 50). For Dewey, dependence is a necessary condition for *interdependence,* which is a powerful ally for a learner of any age. Without interdependence, and with too much independence, you will disregard what others offer as their experience, or what they can contribute to your understanding of a subject. This can lead to indifference. While an indifferent learner, according to the definitions so far, is a contradiction in terms, becoming an indifferent teacher is tantamount to failure.

If one were to combine the ideas of Knowles and Dewey, the andragogical framework that recognizes the importance of experience would suggest that optimal adult learning is transformative learning. According to Jack Mezirow (1991), transformative learning includes the reinterpretation of experiences, old or new, as seen through a new set of expectations that ". . . give a new meaning and perspective to an old experience" (1991, 11). In order for adults to learn, they must sort through prior experience, also known as frames of reference (Mezirow 1997), to determine what aspects of the new experience are relevant and are important to making a new interpretation overall.

These frames of reference define one's lived experience. Frames of reference are also seen as the consequences of cultural assimilation and the influences of those charged with raising the child into adulthood. Mezirow breaks these frames of reference into two facets: habits of mind and points of view. He defines habits of mind as "broad, abstract, orienting, habitual ways of thinking, feeling, and acting influenced by assumptions that constitute a set of codes" (1997, 6). For Mezirow, points of view grow out of habits of mind but are more open to change and can be evaluated using another's point of view. Most college settings offer you the opportunity to learn from your experiences and to develop new habits of learning, building upon or constructing new habits. Specifically, through the process of having a mentoring relationship and your reflection upon it, you will be able to make the most of your teacher training.

It is important to include here the varied ways in which culture has influenced your learning style. From a sociocultural viewpoint, you must remember that all learning occurs in a social context (Vygotsky 1978). Our dispositions and habits are shaped by these influences and will impact our relationships with mentors, peers, and children alike.

In addition, the andragogical framework suggests that adults need informational as well as transformational knowledge. Sandra Kerka (2001) summarizes Kegan's (2000) ideas about informational and transformational knowledge. Informational knowledge might include "learning about money, time, and stress management . . . becoming informed about flextime and childcare options . . . learning related to work/ life issues. Such learning is 'aimed at increasing our fund of knowledge, at increasing our repertoire of skills, at extending already established cognitive capacities into new terrain'" (2001, 48).

Transformational learning, on the other hand, seeks to change how we know, "altering our existing frame of reference, [and] our ways of making meaning" (Kerka 2001, 3). Within the mentoring relationship, you would hope for information that could make your daily experience at work and in school easier. But ultimately, you would do better to have learning experiences and guidance in the form of transformational knowledge. As early childhood educators, we know how offering a wider range of approaches and broader applications allows children opportunities to build upon previous understandings and to construct their own knowledge about a subject and its content. The same can be said for the mentored adult learner, except that the adult learner is able to conscientiously analyze those learning experiences.

Mentoring as an Integral Part of Learning to Become a Teacher

Mentoring is a key component of teacher education programs because people learn best through experience and by reflecting on that experience. As an early childhood teacher, I found that to be true for children, and as a teacher educator, I have found it to be true for aspiring teachers.

I have always believed that much of what we practice in exemplary early childhood classrooms should be offered as models of education for older children and adults alike. For example, as is the practice in early childhood classrooms, the presence of more than one adult not only helps organize and care for many children, it actually gives the adults themselves ways to see things that they may have missed noticing if they were alone. Whether you are discussing observations of children, developing flow charts around curricular ideas using brain-storming techniques, or interfacing with specialists to meet individual children's needs, separately and collectively, these practices all add up to having more profound insight into your work.

Dialogue, the human way of reaching understanding with another, is shared communication that is based on a "universal core of basic attitudes, a tacit consensus about norms and values and fundamental rules" (Mezirow 1991, 65). In the case of the mentored relationship, dialogues must hold aspects of each other's meanings and experiences as well as those definitions or norms that are shared in order for each participant to reach his or her separate and/or common goals. Using this model, wouldn't it be to your benefit to explore the possibilities that enriching exchanges with knowledgeable others, in this case, mentors, could provide?

Good mentoring is essential to becoming a good teacher; the two roles mirror and support one another. According to Maryann Jacobi (1991), the function of mentors is to put courage into their protégés by inciting and motivating them. Isn't that what good teachers do for children? Just as good teaching incites the learner to ask questions, explore and experiment, reflect on and revisit aspects of an experience and probe suppositions, good mentoring should encourage the same. Good mentoring will help you to believe that you are capable of succeeding in college by taking responsibility for your own learning through active participation in the college community of learners, that you have a right to a place in that community, and that you will claim that place and the voice that goes with it.

As good early childhood educators know, it is imperative that we start where children are, making use of the knowledge they bring to the care/education setting from their homes, communities, and cultures. The skilled mentor of adults will use your initiative and your wealth of experience to help you shape your transformative journey.

Good teachers also know that their role is to support the learner without taking over the learning experience by commanding that the learner "know" without true understanding. Aside from the content knowledge that you hope to learn, the mentored relationship can be thought of as an experience in and of itself. Staying true to a constructivist approach, the adult mentoring relationship will provide opportunities for experiential learning and scaffolding so that you take on increasingly difficult tasks.

When I was a classroom teacher, one of the highlights of the school year came when the assistant teacher and I could sit back and watch the class function without us. Enough time had gone by so that the children felt safe in their shared understandings of each other, of class rules, and of the materials. This doesn't mean that we shirked responsibility or that this revelatory observation lasted longer than a few minutes. But what I was looking for was the children's ownership of their classroom. And when I recognized it, I knew the children had in place the mechanisms to be lifelong learners.

In a successful mentoring relationship in which you thrive by sharing and making meaning with others in the university, you will have to cultivate a sense of responsibility for your own learning. The difference here is that you will also be responsible for reflecting on that learning. For Mezirow, the adult must practice critical reflection as the most significant learning experience embedded within transformative learning

(1990). Mezirow also relies on John Dewey's definitions of reflection and calls this validity testing. He quotes Dewey's pragmatic approach to reflective thought in the context of problem solving as "active, persistent and careful consideration of any belief or supposed form of knowledge in the light of the grounds that support it and the further conclusion to which it tends" (Dewey 1933, 9, as cited in Mezirow 1991, 100). This means that you should be concerned with how reliable or valid a belief is and to what degree it should be accepted or practiced. For Mezirow, reflection includes "a review of the way we have consciously, coherently and purposefully applied ideas in strategizing and implementing each phase of solving a problem" (1991, 101).

As we shall see in Chapter 2, critically reflective learning actually includes more than just strategies used to be reflective. Reflective learning and, therefore, transformative learning are not necessarily always rational. Instead, reflective learning is comprised of intuition, other ways of knowing, and empathy (Belenky, Clinchy, Goldberger, and Tarule 1997; Brookfield 1995). Critical reflection includes aspects of cultural contexts that impact upon one's values, beliefs, emotions, and other nonrational and unconscious drives. When you critically reflect, you are also considering why you did what you did. According to Dewey, it is through reflection that we are able to see beyond our habits of mind and our everyday interpretations of experience, taking ourselves to places where we can look back on our learning and actions, and then go beyond them, as it were. Through "speculative questioning" (Brookfield 1995) we offer ourselves options just by having posed the question.

Besides intuitive aspects of reflection, you must also be aware of sociocultural influences on adult transformative learning. These forces often dictate who shall speak and who shall be heard, and who is expected to remain silent, distorting discourse so that what you learn would certainly be qualitatively different if everyone were to fully participate (Mezirow 1996). As adult learners who bring your own meanings from your own experiences to the classroom and the mentored relationship, you should also be aware that many of these same social constructs may impact the way interactions and discourse are carried out in early childhood settings.

Social norms, as seen through the lens of historical and cultural relationships, have played, and continue to play, important roles in your individual beliefs, values, attitudes, and feelings. These influences permeate all aspects of adult learning, including the ways you will construct meaning, how you will go about validity testing, and what that means when you bring theory and practice together in the classroom with children, in adult classrooms, and with your mentor. To take responsibility after reflection is to act with an aim, with an end, and with a vision.

Being responsible and reflecting on experience imply that you are interested in a particular event or subject. In this instance the events are the quality of your mentoring relationship and your teaching experiences. The subject is you.

That said, how could you not be interested?

Benefiting from the Mentoring Relationship

How mentoring and good teaching mirror, support, and parallel one another and how being mentored helps you become a conscientious teacher

❖ A Humanistic Approach to Mentoring
❖ Mentoring as a Transformative Experience
❖ Reflective Practices
❖ Being Reflexive as You Learn and Teach
❖ Being Reflexive in the Mentoring Relationship

A Humanistic Approach to Mentoring

Many teacher education programs are currently undergoing external reviews for accreditation and are therefore required to not only define and describe in more and more somewhat unvarying terms what teachers should know, the skills that are important for every teacher to have, and which types of temperament and character are acceptable, but also to articulate mentoring roles and responsibilities that will result in teachers demonstrating these skills and dispositions. Norman and Ganser (2004, 131) note that "mentor programs increasingly are subject to external influences in much the same way that teaching is influenced by high-stakes achievement testing for children." And they caution against these "formally organized and implemented programs that are largely contrived and artificially constructed" (2004, 131).

For the early childhood world this also means being left out of the jargon of these texts and assessment protocols. For example, in these texts, adult students are called "candidates," and children are called "students." If we are expected to use this terminology in our daily conversations with each other and with our mentors, how can we remain true to early childhood philosophies that value young children's learning outside of traditional teacher/learner relationships? If mentors themselves begin to use jargon that disregards the tenets of early childhood educational philosophy, how will this affect the mentoring relationship? And what are we to do about children who may be older than the early learner, are identified as students, yet need more time still to be children?

Therefore, in taking Norman and Ganser's caution to heart, a quality mentoring relationship should take on more of the characteristics of early childhood education with its learner-centered approach, and combine that with what adult educators say about shared experience, making meaning, and seeing the world from another's perspective, in other words, a humanistic approach to teaching and mentoring.

A humanistic approach to mentoring stands in contrast to standardized, interpersonal relationships between the mentor and mentees. The humanist philosophy comes from theories of psychology advanced by Carl Rogers (1951) who proposed client-centered therapy in which the patient's feelings and viewpoints are validated in the course of developing healthy ways to deal with the world.

This approach, often used in counseling, is well suited as a model of mentoring for those in the teaching profession. Early childhood educators use this approach often in the classroom. We validate a child's feelings and reflect them back using descriptive language and offering alternative ways to approach the problem: "I know it seems difficult, but it's something you'll learn to do" or "It's OK to be angry, but it's not OK to hurt your friend." While it's impossible for anyone to know what another feels, this ability to listen, mirror, and give words to the mentee's emotional state, and offer alternative ways to express emotions, is a valuable attribute in a good mentor. And it models what we should be doing in the classroom as teachers.

Along these lines, the mentor in a humanistic mentee-centered relationship should help you make connections between your feelings, your attitudes, and your behaviors in relation to your own development or your teaching performance. A good mentor may ask that you share stories or narratives to help contextualize your current perspectives with the purpose of "helping [you] unpack [your] perceptions, piecing them together again in a fashion that enhances [your] professional life" (Norman and Ganser 2004, 136).

One of the fundamental tenets of counseling based on humanistic psychology is that "each individual has the possibility for creative attainment of his or her potential" (Norman and Ganser 2004, 133). Humanistic counseling works toward this potential through client-centered therapy. According to Kelly (1997, cited in Norman and Ganser 2004), the core of humanistic therapy is for the counselor to bring a sense of "empathy, positive regard, and genuineness" (1997, 133) to the relationship. In a humanistic approach to mentoring, and to working with young children, emotions are validated. In a humanistic approach to mentoring teacher candidates, the mentor will help you understand that you are not expected to perform perfectly or to perform from a preconceived notion of what good teaching looks like. Although good mentors are able to see good teaching when it happens, different people look for different things. Remember, most mentors in education settings are or have been teachers themselves. They should understand when you are unsure or hesitant about your work. At the same time, you should be prepared to think about your work, and to discuss it critically.

Allison

During a teacher-support group meeting, Allison, a new teacher of second grade children, told of the difficulty she was having with one particular child. She began by describing this child, Rodger, as being one grade behind in his reading, being disruptive and ill-kempt, and being "bussed" to school. Allison focused on what she saw as the task at hand: controlling his behavior so that she could teach him to read. She seemed frustrated and even spoke of being powerless to help this child.

In order to learn more about this child, the group asked questions, most of which had nothing to do with Rodger's academic skills. As the group pieced the puzzle together, they realized that for Rodger, learning to read was the least of his problems. Rodger's mother had succumbed to a long illness and had died some months back.

The group helped this new teacher put Rodger's behaviors in context, asking her to think about why he may be "acting out." Most importantly, they helped her to recognize her own expectations and emotions. She came to see her frustration at not being able to "teach" Rodger as only the top layer of what she was truly feeling. Her major frustration was that she was not getting any help from the administration or this child's family. When the group asked her what she thought *he* was feeling, they were surprised by how much of her response resonated with what her own feelings were: frustration and a deep sense of impotence. Being able to name her own emotions and to empathize with this child helped her to see what she needed to do next. Shifting her paradigm from "this child is trouble" to "this child is troubled" helped her to see the need to deepen her relationship with him, to support his accomplishments, and to continue to advocate for his well-being.

- What types of questions might you ask this teacher to help her see the whole child?
- What aspects of this child's story are being left out?
- In what ways could you help this teacher reflect on her own emotions?
- What types of supports might you suggest she seek out?

A humanistic approach to early childhood classrooms also puts the child, and often the family, at the center of the learning environment. By facilitating the child's learning and providing opportunities to explore interests, teachers bring together child-centered practices with observations of individual children's behaviors. It is in putting this information together that the good teacher attempts to understand the whole child and the group. Again, perfection or instant understanding is not the goal. It is in the experiencing and reflecting that one learns deeply.

According to a teacher-centered model of mentoring, the good mentor will not only assess your skills as a prospective teacher and your ability to teach, he or she will also ask about and reflect upon the quality of your college experience. The mentor will be concerned with your struggles with professional identity and your sense of yourself as an active and empowered learner. If these qualitative aspects of the mentoring experience are lost in a system where mentoring takes place in deference to external standards and student performance outcomes, Norman and Ganser (2004, 133) fear that mentoring is "in danger of losing its soul."

Therefore, as you would expect to find within holistic, child-centered early care/education settings, you should find empathy, nurturance, guidance, flexibility, and patience within a framework of humanistic mentoring.

Mentoring as a Transformative Experience

As you move through your mentored relationship, your teacher education program, and your development as an early childhood practitioner, you will pass through different stages of professional development. In 1972, Lillian Katz devised a way of looking at the stages of development that a preschool teacher goes through as she moves toward mastery of her profession. Although there are some questions about the number of stages involved, Katz proposed that the complexity of your learning and teaching increases as you develop toward becoming a mature early childhood educator. The following are stages of preschool teacher development according to Lillian Katz (1972):

Stage 1: *The Survival Stage:* This stage is characterized by the phrase "What do I do on Monday?" The teacher is mainly preoccupied with daily realities of classroom life such as activity-based curriculum and management, including schedules, behavior, and parent/teacher relationships.

Stage 2: *The Consolidation Stage:* This stage most often occurs during the second or third year of teaching. Here the teacher is able to bring together and examine the skills she has gained from the experiences of the first year. She can put her energies toward focusing on individual children and consider which other specific skills she would like to master, for example, observation and recording techniques.

Stage 3: *The Renewal Stage:* This stage occurs in the third and fourth year of teaching. In this stage, the teacher may become tired of doing the same things and looks for new and innovative practices and information in the field of early childhood education and care.

Stage 4: *The Maturity Stage:* This stage usually begins after three or more years of teaching. Here the teacher is squarely situated in her practice. She sees herself as a professional, and the questions she asks are usually deeper and more philosophical. She also begins to take on leadership roles, for example, hosting student teachers or mentoring a new teacher or a peer.

Karen Vander Ven also named stages in early childhood teachers' development. She differs from Katz's descriptions in that she lists ways that teachers should be supervised at each stage. The following are stages of preschool teachers' professional development and accompanying supervision according to Vander Ven (1988):

Stage 1: *The Novice Stage:* The novice teacher has the minimum education necessary for her position and requires a high level of direct supervision. This person often considers issues from the viewpoint of her own personal experience.

Stage 2: *The Initial Stage:* The teacher in the initial stage has more training and may decide to stay in the field. While she also needs direct supervision, since she is thinking of staying, she is open to it.

Stage 3: *The Informed Stage:* The teacher in the informed stage is committed to teaching, and therefore has at least a bachelor's degree. This teacher uses appropriate practices, including an understanding of working with families. Along with her commitment comes a sense of autonomy, although she will participate in supervision willingly.

Stage 4: *The Complex Stage* and Stage 5: *The Influential Stage:* Teachers in these stages take on leadership roles and supervise other teachers. Often, their work influences others in the field.

Teachers in stages 3, 4, and 5 will most likely be your mentors in cooperative settings.

In their book, *The Early Childhood Mentoring Curriculum,* Dan Bellm, Marcy Whitebook, and Patty Hnatiuk (1997) suggest that mentors should be knowledgeable about and understand each individual practitioner's development. The authors generalize teachers' growth in terms of the ability to become less self-centered in order to be more child-centered, more confident, and able to call on and use varied teaching strategies, including evaluating individual children's needs and applying appropriate strategies to meet these diverse needs. These authors speak about the mature teacher's ability to see beyond her or his own classroom to understand child care and education as a larger profession. This professional stance guides educators to become responsible to philosophical, moral, and policy imperatives.

Bellm, Whitebook and Hnatiuk (1997) also address the emotional needs of new teachers. They understand that with good mentoring the new teacher should move from a sense of isolation to collegiality; that she will recognize her own strengths and successes while at the same time identifying areas that still need to be developed. The new teacher will learn to cope with stress and manage time productively. And, importantly, she will learn how to participate in self-evaluation, developing the ability to work with a supervisor and respond constructively to his or her evaluations in order to continue to develop professionally.

Therefore, it will be important for you to understand that your mentor should be mindful of these stages of professional development. Your mentor should also help you identify which stage you are in, so that you do not expect yourself to perform in ways that you are not yet ready to realize.

In a study conducted by Arlene Martin and June Trueax in 1997, early childhood teachers and their mentors reported that they had undergone personal and professional transformation as a result of having had a mentoring relationship. By examining how early childhood teachers perceived mentoring, the researchers interviewed mentors and mentees and discovered that, for both, the most important aspects of the mentored relationship included trust, openness and acceptance, support, and encouragement. These dimensions were not bound to stages of teachers' professional growth and could appear at any point in the development of a relationship.

Martin and Trueax (1997) discuss periods most common to the mentoring relationships they studied. For the teachers in this study, the most important feature in the *relationship-building period* was *trust.* Trust developed as they began their relationship by spending time together, getting to know one another.

As the relationship progressed, the mentor's *knowledge* of child development, developmentally appropriate practices, and instruction were paramount. The teachers reported that the mentor's skill, knowledge, and expertise in early childhood education became more important as the team moved into a period for *building an agenda* for supervision.

In order to build an *information exchange,* the next period of the relationship fostered the development of ways to communicate so that both people in the relationship could feel comfortable. The authors found that the degree to which the mentee was able to receive feedback and the quality of her reflections had a pronounced effect on the intensity and the authenticity of the relationship.

In the next period, *laying the groundwork for change* moved the pair toward a mature relationship. This was characterized by a more collegial attitude and gave each person more opportunities to take on broader responsibilities. The deeper levels of intensity and authenticity, which were influenced by the quality of the mentee's reflections, in turn directly influenced how quickly the mentoring relationship developed.

Finally, the roles that had defined the initial relationship changed. The relationship *moved to transformation* and came to a close. The mentor pushed and empowered

---

Box 2-1

A definition of mentoring

Martin and Trueax (1997) found five themes that both the mentors and protégés felt were part of a definition of mentoring. These include

- Mentoring builds a foundation for growth and change.
- Mentoring promotes personal development.
- Mentoring promotes professional growth.
- Mentoring changes both mentors and protégés.
- Mentoring provides benefits to both mentors and protégés.

---

the protégé toward *risk and vision,* and both stepped into the roles of friends and colleagues. It is important to understand that through the dimensions of empowerment, risk, and vision, both you and your mentor will undergo personal and professional transformations and will most likely connect as colleagues rather than as teacher and student.

While the above themes may seem to be rather generalized statements, they reflect the actual experiences reported by the mentors and protégés in this study. Further, the authors suggest that both the mentors and protégés "gained increased self-confidence and self-esteem and improved their practice. Each mentor and protégé recommitted to remain in the field of early childhood, renewed their professional interests, sought higher professional goals, and became more career-directed with interests in the areas of advocacy and leadership" (Martin and Trueax 1997, 49).

Martin and Trueax's article specifically focuses on the positive impacts of mentoring on early childhood teachers. In their summation, they compare the best aspects of the mentor/protégé relationship with the caring and nurturance within a teacher/child relationship or parent/child relationship. I, too, strongly believe that early childhood education models are valuable to the educational world at large, and that much of our pedagogy should be "pushed up," rather than skills-based learning continuously being forced "down." Martin and Trueax's comment that "the nature of the mentoring relationship provides a powerful, intimate role that matches the nature of the early childhood professional within his or her work setting" (1997, 51) goes straight to the heart of this book. Culturally and developmentally appropriate teaching and learning through experience and reflection are excellent models for adult education and mentoring relationships alike.

Reflective Practices

When you decide to attend college, you are already engaged in reflection and self-efficacy. Everyone brings prior knowledge and experience to the university classroom, and since some of that experience and knowledge is often qualitatively different from the cannon of historically accepted "knowledge worth knowing," you must actively demand that your voice and your needs be recognized and satisfied.

As Gonzalez Rodriguez and Sjostrom (1998, 177) caution, many students of education, and especially the nontraditional adult student teacher, "may need strategies to help them become conscious of the consequences of their attitudes, beliefs, and rules, long taken for granted, by which they make sense of their world." By using reflective practices in a mentoring relationship, you can come to rely on "structures that facilitate questioning whether [your] traditional ways of doing things produce the results [you] want to achieve in [your] teaching" (1998, 177). Therefore, in thinking about those traditional ways of doing things, it will be helpful for you to reflect on and question the methods, attitudes, and outcomes of your own schooling and education as well.

Reflection

According to Donald Schön, whose important work *The Reflective Practitioner* (1983) gave the teaching profession ways to look at what he called our "professional artistry," teachers must develop an ability to see themselves in the act of teaching. Schön described components of this artistry as *reflection-in-action* and *reflection-on-action*. Reflection-in-action is the ability to think analytically about something *while* it is happening. This ability is one of the hallmarks of good teaching. To be able to think about something while it is happening allows you to immediately adjust your behaviors or your interactions. Good teachers can do this while they are working with children, getting feedback from the learner, and adjusting the experience to scaffold learning and meet the child's needs.

Reflection-on-action is the next layer, as it were, to reflection-in-action. Since all actions come to an end at some point, to become a good teacher you must reflect on what you did during the action in the first place. Being able to review your practices using reflection-in-action lets you to think about what worked, what didn't work, and what could be done better next time. Thinking about and acting on your work with others will make you a better teacher and a better student.

According to Hyun and Marshall (1997), who wrote about developmentally and culturally appropriate practices in early childhood education, effective reflective practices also include

- A *cognitive element*. This aspect of reflection occurs when you use wide-ranging principles to make connections across disciplines. The cognitive element in reflection is strongest when you combine the subject you are studying with "the most personal form of reflective practice—the 'inner dialogue'" (129).
- A *narrative element*, which occurs when you tell your own story, putting your individual "experience into context . . . [thus] providing a much richer understanding of what takes place" (129).
- A *critical element of reflection*, which is evident when you engage your ability to "analyze different . . . perspectives" so that you can include others' experiences and perspectives in order to "understand and properly act on . . . inconsistencies" (129).

Hyun and Marshall also coined the term, *reflection-for-action*, referring to your concerted efforts to direct your energies toward change. In practicing *reflection-for-action*, you will be assuming a political stance, since, for the critically reflective learner and educator, it will most likely include challenges to the status quo.

The ability to be reflective will help you to develop a truly productive relationship with your mentor. In using a reflective stance you will be able to assess both your behaviors and your understanding, your responses and your ability to negotiate, and your desire to look forward and plan for rich and productive learning experiences. Reflection therefore also includes looking forward.

If you think about it, these elements are also valuable for the undergraduate in any academic concentration.

Critical Reflection

Although Dewey's (1919/1958) and Schön's (1983) ideas about experience and reflective practices bring together ways to help teachers become aware of their thoughts and actions, either while they are occurring, after the fact, or when planning for the future, these theories are based on individual experiences, and therefore individual solutions. There is a concern that this kind of reflection doesn't go far to address the *context* in which teaching occurs.

According to Brookfield (1995), teachers who engage in critical reflection use new ways to think about established beliefs and values held by society. Teachers who engage in critically reflective practices consider multiple perspectives and continually question their own and others' assumptions (Gonzalez Rodriguez, and Sjostrom 1998). Critically reflective teachers consider the broader implications of schooling and education. As a critically reflective teacher, you will be encouraged to focus on the political as well as the personal components of your work, and to take action to promote change, equity, and social justice. As a critically reflective teacher, you and your mentor will work together to challenge not only the tenets of early childhood principles and practices, but will challenge each other to broaden and share experience and meanings.

One of the unresolved issues related to mentoring is "What is the correct balance between guiding mentees to maintain the status quo and encouraging them to create change and transformation?" (Kochan and Pascarelli 2003, *x*). As a critically reflective teacher and learner, you will come to understand that this question does not only have to do with individual transformation and change, but can also be taken to mean seeing yourself as a change agent in your center, school, university classroom, or within your larger community. For example, many teachers whose experiences and perspectives already differ from the status quo often question such inequities of educational settings asking, "Who gets what kinds of education?" or "Why are early childhood educators historically paid less than elementary education teachers?" Since these types of questions will no doubt come up as you develop critical and reflective skills, you may find the following organizational tools, stemming from notions of critical theory and critical pedagogy, helpful.

Although critical theory is certainly much more detailed than I will describe here, Barry Kanpol (1999, 1) offers a succinct and relevant definition, seeing critical theory as "a form of thought and action to challenge the dominant and oppressive ideologies constructed historically." Working with a critically reflective mentor can help you to also think critically about how learning and teaching occur, how they reflect avenues of power, and how these are revealed in different contexts.

As Kanpol points out, by participating in an educational setting, it is assumed that you have identified yourself as a student and you are essentially motivated to learn. By choosing to attend college, you are, by and large, intrinsically motivated to become better educated. Yet Kanpol (1999) distinguishes between "education" and "schooling," seeing schooling as a mechanism for social control through social class distinctions. According to Kanpol, schooling takes on a role as a socialization agent, focusing on management and control as a way to support an economy that needs workers and managers.

Many children and adults who have gone through public education systems have been deskilled; that is, they are expected to learn in environments in which they lack autonomy, have no power to make decisions about their learning, and are then held accountable for someone else's mandates (Kanpol 1998). For example, standardized, timed, and often scripted curriculum will most likely put the needs of the individual learner last. If you are expected to keep to timetables and teach to the test, authoritarian control can become a necessary objective. From this viewpoint, Rodger, the child described previously, would be seen as a failure because he did not perform in a preconceived manner at a given time. This way of looking at what he could not do, known as the deficit model, labeled him as not ready. Instead, using a critically reflective approach, you would need to assess what he could do and ask how to make the school ready for him.

As a critically reflective teacher, you would find it impossible to practice deskilling. You would instead practice reskilling, demanding that those you teach become critically reflective learners. Using this approach, you would put knowledge of a subject in context and rather than teach to the test (schooling), you would use knowledge in broader, less formulaic, and more transformative ways (education).

Reskilling has the ability to transform schooling into education. Barry Kanpol (1998, 9) offers this way of looking at the situation:

> To begin the "critical" project is to simultaneously be reflective on how one is
> personally schooling oneself and their clientele, while also attempting to move out of
> the schooling mentality, both theoretically and practically . . . we can indeed educate
> our students (and, I believe, ourselves) if we choose when and where it is appropriate
> to resist schooling structures.

As a critically reflective educator/learner you will address issues such as racism, social class-based assumptions, and gender and ability stereotypes not only in your own learning (mentored relationships and college classrooms) but as they become evident in the education and lives of others, especially the young children you will teach. Again, in the struggle to overcome control, authoritarianism, individualism, deskilling, and traditional literacy paradigms (Kanpol 1998), you will have to peel away, examine, and question many layers of experience, not the least of which will be your own "schooling."

Reflecting on your own educational experiences will not only be practical, it will help you to sort out the ways that you were taught and the ways you learned, including the emotions you felt in different educational settings. These memories often point to assumptions we have about teachers and teaching, and about children and ourselves as learners. Many education students, regardless of the time spent in teacher education courses, teach the way they were taught, which makes sense since you were a student for many more years than you are a teacher. And for many pre-service teachers, especially students who may not have attended child-centered classrooms, ideas about teaching are often significantly different from what the current early childhood professional associations consider appropriate practices (Bredekamp and Copple 1997).

Who gets what kind of *schooling* is largely decided by those whose philosophies reinforce the existing social class distinctions. These distinctions and educational outcomes are easily seen, especially in public school settings (Kozol 1991). Demanding to be educated will depend on your ability to become a critically reflective learner who welcomes change and is genuinely motivated to learn (Kanpol 1998). Paolo Freire (1973) calls on students and teachers to become partners in problem-posing and investigation. He believes that it is in the act of discourse that teachers and students come to share understandings about each other's experiences and about each other's understandings of those experiences by way of discourse. His teaching method recommends "1) identifying and naming the problem, 2) analyzing the causes of the problem, and 3) finding solutions to the problem" (cited in Sleeter 1996, 117).

By using a critically reflective paradigm, you will become interested in examining the structure of schools, including the history and sociology of early childhood education, local and national child care and education policy, local and national bureaucracies, standardization and regulation of curricula and teaching methods, and the co-option of early childhood practices through regulation. Critically reflective mentors and protégés recognize the power of learning from an authoritative voice, as compared to being schooled by someone who holds authoritarian control. Wielding or succumbing to hierarchies of power should be replaced with sharing a deeper respect for one another's knowledge and development. Imagine the capacity for deeper learning when each participant's learning is valued.

Being a critically reflective practitioner, you will come to recognize adult and young learners as authorities of their own cultures. You will also value the give-and-take of new knowledge in the relationship and use others' expertise as a way to make and share meaning, especially in culturally and linguistically diverse settings. But you must be cautious not to fall into the trap of individualistic or centrist attitudes. These views can separate you from your learning community, creating a competitive or oppositional and divisive atmosphere. In order for you to become expert at critical reflection, your mentor, who should recognize what you bring to the table including your individual styles and needs, will help you to reflect on your beliefs, attitudes, and ability to hear and appreciate others.

Christina - Part I

The building that Christina taught in was almost 100 years old. It was part of the church that she had attended as a child in this close-knit Puerto Rican community in Manhattan. When her own children were young, they went to this same school, and Christina became involved with the PTA. Years later, she asked the principal for a job and was assigned a fifth grade class. Since this was a parochial school, she did not need a license. But Christina felt she didn't have a right to teach children without knowing something about teaching. She enrolled in a public community college and took courses in the only education program they had—early childhood education.

After Christina graduated from the community college, she continued going to school, working toward her B.S. in early childhood. When it was time for Christina to do her student teaching placement, she was allowed to teach in her own classroom. But she would have to change grades and work with younger children.

Christina worked it out with her principal to move to the second grade. When we met at the beginning of the school year Christina told me, "You wouldn't believe it! What a mess! I spent three days during the summer just cleaning out the classroom! There were books—textbooks and readers—from thirty years ago. I must have thrown away ten pounds of old mimeographed papers. I put up all the pictures that my principal said had to go up for the first day of school and I arranged the desks in groups instead of rows. But I'm not so sure about this second-grade-thing. I don't think I'm gonna like it. They're so little and they're gonna need so much attention."

When I came to see her classroom, I was taken aback by just how traditional everything actually was. The children were quietly bent over their workbooks as Christina walked around the room checking their homework. The pictures that she spoke about were all mass-produced. They included drawings of holiday celebrations that portrayed Christopher Columbus and his three ships, a Native American and a Pilgrim child holding vegetables, a witch on a broomstick, and more. There were also mass-produced lists of word families with blank lines waiting to be filled in, and a word wall consisting of vocabulary words that the teacher's edition of the reader suggested. The shelves did indeed hold many books, but most of them were all the same: texts for math, science, or social studies. What there was of a library shelf, held a few tattered children's storybooks.

The children were sitting in rows and when I asked her about this, she said, "Oh, the principal and the other teachers didn't like what I did and said I had to put it back, that if I had the tables in groups in my class, the kids in the other classes might want to know why they couldn't sit together also."

Cristina and I met a few days later for our first reflection. She said she had so many ideas for her classroom but was despondent since other teachers were giving her a hard time about any changes she wanted to make. She started talking about specific children and wanted me to tell her "what to do with them."

Instead, I asked her to tell me what she thought were the children's strengths. Christina immediately answered "They are so well behaved and polite. They ask me if they could do the slightest thing." She thought for a minute and added, "I think this is also a weakness, since I'd like to see them be more independent. They even ask me what they should draw. Now, that breaks my heart."

So I asked her how she could use their strengths, since behavior management didn't seem to be a problem. "Well, I feel like they already know the rules, but I don't want to be the one who decides every little thing. I'd like to see them be able to interact more, maybe work in groups. I'd like to give them more space to move around in and more time to be creative." Christina looked at me and smiled, "I guess I'm even thinking about what they're missing. It seems so hard to separate these things."

During that meeting I also asked her what she thought of the pictures that were on the walls. She said, "They're OK. They just show the holidays." I said, "I wonder what messages the children are getting from these pictures, and the fact that their own work, the drawings of their families, was relegated to one small space on the back wall."

Christina said, "I know. Everything's so old-fashioned. I feel like I'm supposed to be a teacher just like the ones I had . . . you know, everything *I say* goes, and everything *I say* is what they should know. But I know that's not what I think. I really believe that kids should learn what they're interested in learning—even if I do have a curriculum I have to follow. I'm sure we could do what we have to for second grade and still learn it through their interests. I'd like to figure out some way for them to stop waiting for me to tell them what to learn."

I asked her to tell me about the culture of the children's families in her class. We spoke about the traditional schooling most of the parents must have had, especially those who were recent immigrants, and how they probably felt comfortable with the ways the teachers in this school taught their children. Christina said, "Yeah, I know, I'm going to have to think about how to reach out to these families—to show them that I'm not slacking off when I let the children move around the room, or allow them to choose a subject they'd like to find out about." We also spoke about how she would have to make a special effort to develop a trusting relationship with the parents of two children who seemed to need more of her attention.

- What advice might you have for Christina as she tries to enact a more progressive approach to teaching and learning in this traditional setting?
- Consider how you would approach the other teachers in your center or school if they wanted input into your classroom practices.
- Think about what you would need to know about the cultures of the families in this school so that you might develop positive relationships with them, especially if you were planning on enacting changes in the ways their children were taught.
- Who might you ask for help or support before you approach the families of the children that Christina is concerned about? How would you conduct this conference?

Reflexive Practices

In the course of writing this book, I recalled a conversation I had with a colleague in which the subject of reflective practices arose. At the time, she responded that she would rather speak about *reflexivity* and not *reflection*. Truthfully, I wasn't familiar with this concept and it took a bit of research and reading on my part to understand what she meant. Actually, since what I have been trying to say about critical reflection is part of the definition of reflexivity, I think it is important to explore this broader concept not only as a significant aspect of the mentoring relationship, but as an essential skill for adult learners in general.

The definitions of reflexivity are varied depending upon which discipline is addressing it. For sociologists, reflexivity occurs when you are aware of the place (situation) and time (historic period) of the interaction or event, and consciously relate it to "the space of one's point of view" (Bourdieu and Waquant 1992; Kenway and McLeod 2004, 526). In other words, reflexivity occurs when everyone's lived experiences (for example, socioeconomic class, gender, or race) are considered relevant in light of where (for example, classroom or street corner) and when (for example, current political climate or social mores) the interaction takes place.

For educators, reflexivity is learning that is influenced by specific settings. Peter Hoffman-Kipp, Alfredo Artiles, and Laura Lopez-Torres (2003, 3) describe this approach to reflection as "the *shared* nature of reflection through situated activity, reflection as a *social endeavor,* and reflection as a *distributed process*" (italics added). Here, reflexivity is enacted during discussions that bring people together to consider the situation. All members of the group are conscious of who is present, who is speaking, and who is silent. Everyone in the group should also have an opportunity to examine the materials used in the reflection, for example, journals, evaluation methods, materials, or curriculum. This will help you to contextualize and "collaborate, use artifacts, strategize solutions to problems, and rely on other more experienced members . . ." (Hoffman-Kipp et al. 2003, 4). This means that teachers *share* what they are thinking.

Reflection becomes *distributed;* that is, reflection is influenced by others' input and is not just an individual activity as proposed by Schön or Dewey. Therefore, it is important for the entire group to keep in mind the ways that habits and assumptions, personal experiences with deskilled schooling or emancipatory education, and the influence of those in power within or over the group affect the actual work of the *social endeavor* of the learning community. As you engage with and share your reflections with other teachers, as well as with your mentor, you will be bringing personal reflective practices, critical reflection, and situated learning together.

Reflexivity is also considered a way to think about your life story. It is the process by which you "self-consciously and reflexively construct [your] identity" (Kenway and McLeod 2004, 526). Participating in reflexive relationships, like critical reflection, will require that you question your experiences in relation to sociocultural, institutional, and historical contexts. Roles that you may believe are established and fixed will change as you strive to understand how personal goals, learning practices, and context interact (Edwards, Ranson, and Strain 2002).

In order to develop and continue to be reflexive, you will need to acknowledge and welcome others through dialogue. You will need to be willing to learn from their perspectives, their dispositions, and their ways of identifying themselves in the world. Elizabeth Tisdell (1998, 150) speaks about the ability to "see with a third eye." By this she means that reflexive practitioners always consider how their understandings and knowledge relate not only to themselves but to others in social contexts and power relations. Janet Gonzalez-Mena (2005), an infant-toddler specialist, also speaks about a "third space" that early childhood teachers can create when they work with parents. She suggests we tolerate differences in perspectives and beliefs, allowing these differences to have their rightful place in discussions, without assigning these differences the power to push each other further apart.

Like individualistic or centrist viewpoints, private and exclusive reflection will not serve you well here. You will need to nurture a capacity to hear others' voices, examine circumstances where some people speak and others remain silent, be open to change, and use available resources to move toward defining who you are and who you are becoming.

For me, education is what you learn throughout your lifetime. It takes place in many different locations and can come from and go in many different directions. In order to claim your place in a democratic society, you will need to claim your right to learn in many venues and from all directions. This is what you can get from working with a mentor and creating a community of learners among your peers.

As your mentoring relationship develops, you will probably begin to think about how to put some of the ideas addressed here into practice. You will also begin to consider ways that these theories can become part of your teaching practices with young children. An excellent source of information that can help you understand what a critical pedagogy in an early childhood classroom might look like can be found in Vivian Maria Vasquez's *Negotiating Critical Literacies with Young Children* (2004). In this book, Vasquez challenges herself and the children in her pre-K classroom to think about, research, and address some of the most common misconceptions about gender roles, materialism, and ecology. The organization and quality of the work they produce are powerful examples and vivid models of critical pedagogies and ways to engage young children in meaningful learning.

While you may go to a particular college, and may be presented with information that is considered important to know as a teacher of young children, there is always more to learn, and always more *ways* to learn about it. Just as good teachers offer children avenues of exploration by asking good questions and pointing out learning, good mentors will help you develop a repertoire of skills for your own learning and show you how to do the same for those you will teach. Just as reflexivity will help you assess the structures and interactions in teacher education settings, enacting critical pedagogy will help you guide others to challenge practices and beliefs that benefit only a few and marginalize many.

Being Reflexive as You Learn and Teach

As many teachers of young children know, no one comes to school empty-headed. The idea that educators once had about transferring information onto a tabula rasa has long ago been put aside. Children arrive at preschool and adults arrive at the university with their own familial and cultural frames of reference. Since these familial and cultural reference points are wedded to the way you understand what it means to learn and to teach, being critically reflective in a mentoring relationship should add to your awareness of the mentoring relationship itself.

But you cannot stop there. As part of a community of learners, and in order to broaden your understanding of the work of teachers, you will have to examine the "sociopolitical contexts of teaching in addition to . . . curricular and pedagogical concerns" (Hoffman-Kipp et al. 2003, 250). You should have many opportunities to be reflexive, by not only focusing on individual experiences but by questioning "sign-systems and artifacts that are embedded in the social activity of the school community" (Hoffman-Kipp et al. 2003, 250).

Old paradigms of learning and teaching should be examined as part of a reflexive mentoring relationship. As a new teacher you should be exposed to different early childhood care/education settings so that you can see different approaches to discipline, play, literacy, or adult-child interactions, to name just a few. If you find that you are only seeing a limited repertoire of practices, views, and expectations, and that you want to see other approaches to teaching young children, find out from your mentor or your peers where you would be welcomed to observe. Hopefully, you and your mentor will become comfortable enough in your relationship to discuss issues regarding different practices in different cultural settings. For the prospective early childhood educator, these issues will not only become relevant to your own education but must become central to the work you will do with young children and their families.

Being in reflexive relationships as you learn and teach also means valuing interdependence. In teacher education, it is expected that new teachers will ask for help. This is not a sign that you are less capable than others. In fact, rather than passively letting yourself "be schooled" or not acting until a crisis occurs, asking for help shows that you are empowered to actively engage and learn from those around you.

In order to succeed in a reflexive community, you will need to understand your ability to collaborate, strategize, and rely on others along the way. What you bring to the mentored relationship is the valuable knowledge of your own lived experience, your willingness to learn more, and your eagerness to get started.

Being Reflexive in the Mentoring Relationship

Teaching is considered one of the "helping professions." As someone who will interact with people (as opposed to working with numbers or machines), you will naturally have unpredictable and infinitely varied interactions in your work. What you may plan to do, or what outcomes you may hope for, are going to be influenced by the people involved in your work. It is therefore helpful to develop a reflexive partnership with your mentor, your cooperating teacher, and your peers in order to question your understandings of curriculum, your expectations of children, your opinions about diverse families, and your images of teachers in general and assumptions about other teachers in particular.

It is also important to remember that all learning and communication take place within particular contexts. Remember, the mentor will not always know or be familiar with your work setting. She will need you to be prepared to share information so that she can guide you with greater consideration and purpose. And that is just the reason why you have sought out a mentor in the first place.

Bring your concerns to your mentor. Be honest. If something occurred that was in fact your fault, for example, giving misinformation to a parent, don't try to hide it. It is better to admit a mistake than attempt to cover it up and be found out later.

Don't blame others. Look instead for the root cause of the problem. As a teacher and as a good mentee, you will need to analyze the incident and uncover what role you played, what were inappropriate interactions, who holds what status, and what steps you can take to make the next interaction work for you. Using a reflexive stance with your mentor as you review particular incidents will help prepare you for your next interaction with the person who is giving you cause for concern in the first place.

Being open to praise as well as to critique is an asset in a reflexive mentoring relationship. Many of us are used to deflecting or negating compliments. Being modest is not a bad thing, but don't forget what the compliment was about. Value this recognition and understand that if someone else can see your skill or appreciate your idea, then it is something for you to draw on later. Make a mental note about what it is in particular that you are being recognized for. Is it your writing? Is it your ability to be diplomatic during

---

Box 2-2

Before meeting with your mentor, think about these questions:

- What do I imagine teaching young children to look like?
- What are my expectations for teaching?
- What, if any, inconsistencies have I experienced while teaching or observing others teach?
- What do I think about these inconsistencies?
- How have I handled them?
- What might I like to accomplish during my mentorship that would address some of the conflicts I have experienced between what I am learning as theory and what I observe as practice?

a group discussion? Is it your willingness to share personal stories that add to others' understanding of a topic? Is it that you are in fact humble and yet a leader?

Approach problems professionally. Being in a reflexive mentoring relationship, you should experience an atmosphere in which you can freely talk about your feelings and concerns. Use your meetings to honestly reflect on problems or challenges you face and your responsibility for any of the outcomes. Mentoring experts point out that "the mentor's role is to help you understand your own role and responsibilities, learn to find solutions effectively, and expand your array of skills required to handle various situations that you will encounter throughout your career" (Lee, Theoharis, Fitzpatrick, Kim, Liss, Nix-Williams, Griswold, and Walther Thomas 2006, 235).

It is also recommended that you make a list of the advantages and disadvantages of any solution you and your mentor decide upon (Lee et al. 2003). Using a reflexive stance, you can evaluate and rework solutions in context as you move toward resolving a conflict or a stressful situation. Whether you are working with children or with other adults, being able to reflect-in-action and reflect-on-action will allow you to become your own best resource.

In *Teaching to Mentoring: Principle and Practice, Dialogue and Life in Adult Education* (2004) Professors Lee Herman and Alan Mandell of Empire State College, State University of New York, who have taught and mentored adult students, speak of the "creation of a broadening self" (104) that comes from an ability to "more confidently and deliberately ... discover and present [yourself] as the center of ever-widening circles of curiosity and aspiration: areas of intimacy and leisure, of purely intellectual achievement, of social status, civic commitment and spiritual quest" (103). When reflexive practices become second nature, you will be able to relax and become open to new choices as they present themselves.

Being reflective in your mentored relationships is a behavior that no one else can do for you. Being reflexive in a mentored relationship is a responsibility that should become part of your retinue of active learning techniques. These techniques will serve you far beyond your undergraduate experience. A good mentor should be able to guide you to ask good questions, and in making both practical and academic suggestions, he or she will support you in practicing and refining your techniques, so you can take them with you into the early childhood classroom and the post bachelor's classroom when your mentoring relationship comes to a close.

Establishing a Mentoring Relationship

Ways to begin a relationship

❖ Before You Look for a Mentor

❖ Finding a Mentor

❖ Access Is a Matter of Knowing the Rules: Skills/Strategies Needed to Gain Access to Mentors

❖ Expectations: Yours and Your Mentor's

❖ Characteristics of Good Mentors

❖ Characteristics of Good Mentees

❖ Successful Mentoring Relationships

Before You Look for a Mentor

In many universities, orientations are held for new students. Sometimes these are required as part of an introductory course, other times they are offered on a voluntary basis. They may only take a few hours, or may be scheduled into a noncredit course. If it is required, you must go. If it is voluntary, it is in your best interest to attend. Information about school policies, important dates, applications for various special programs, a tour of the library, and a "heads up" from other students already enrolled are important. Having a picture of what is expected and what is available to you as you begin this new experience makes you all the more effective.

One of the easiest and most productive ways for you to organize your educational goals is to sit with an advisor and begin the process of mapping out an educational trajectory. Knowing your immediate interests will help you develop a short-term schedule of classes you'd like to investigate. Understanding that most courses in a program are sequenced will help you see a long-term plan. While there are times when you may not understand the requirements or sequences offered and you have to ask the advisor to help you sort these out, it is to your benefit when you spend precious time with your advisor to have the rudiments of program planning in place. When you meet your advisor after having done some background work, the conversation starts on a much higher plane—the quality of courses, the professors, the courses that will follow, how you might use this knowledge in the "real" world, and perhaps even some chitchat about your life outside of school.

For example, in your academic life, do you want to be tutored? Do you want to know about scholarships so that you can apply for the ones that match your strengths or needs? Are you interested in a particular aspect of teaching? Do you want information

Box 3-1

The advisor will assume that you have:

- Met the minimum academic standards to have been admitted to the college;
- Read the university catalogue;
- A realistic sense of your academic strengths and weaknesses;
- An understanding of what you can do with the degree;
- Identified what you hope to accomplish in both the academic setting and outside the university (Yarbrough 2002).

about graduate schools that offer a particular program? If an advisor does not know about your particular interests or cannot answer your question, he or she is trained to know where to send you for the answers, including which professors would make a good match for a mentoring relationship.

Besides advisors, faculty, especially those within the department of your major, should not only be available for advisement but should also get to know you personally as you advance through the program. It is often up to you to make that happen. Making contact with your professor may be a little intimidating at first. But even by approaching the professor after class, you will be a student who stands out in the crowd. Think of a particularly interesting point made during the class and talk about it one-on-one. Or, if you are having trouble understanding something, be sure to approach the professor and get clarification. Again, one-on-one time, which can take place during the professor's office hours as well, will help the professor remember you.

Do not wait for a crisis or just before an assignment is due to approach your professors. By being visible, you are paving the way for a mentored relationship. By being visible before a crisis, professors get to see you at your best, or at least from a vantage point that shows you to be proactive, positive, and engaged. As Houser (2005) found, adult learners want instructors to see them as students who take responsibility for their own learning, bring knowledge and experience to the mix, and they want to be treated as adults.

Many college students perceive mentoring to be closely related to tutoring, associating the mentored relationship as only necessary because they need to address weaknesses or deficits (Granados and Lopez 1999). This is, of course, not the only function of the relationship. Even if you know that you have particular academic deficits, the mentoring relationship should be proactive. It should help you develop your strengths as a learner and future teacher.

Finding out about what courses you might be interested in will require that you be an informed consumer.

- You will need to use the *college catalogue.* It is an important source of information, and is an official document. Programs list their requirements, course descriptions, and faculty.
- *Course listings* are quick descriptions of what will be included in the course. Even though these are general descriptions of the major topics to be covered,

there may be slight changes depending on which professor is teaching the course that year.

- The *schedule* will tell you which of the courses that interest you are available that semester. For example, required courses are often offered every semester, but some are not. Meet with your advisor to set up a plan for each year. You don't have to stick to it, but it will help you navigate through registration each semester.

- Go to the *bookstore* and look at the books for the courses that you're interested in taking. See if they match the description of the course and your understanding of the description of the course. Sometimes you might decide to take the course later, or not at all. Sometimes you find you just want to read what's recommended for that course without signing up for it. It's a great way to add to your home library.

- If your school offers *academic advisors,* do not hesitate to use them. These are trained professionals who understand your program, your degree, and your needs. While they may have other duties, they have chosen this profession to serve you.

- *Faculty* members are listed for each department in the college. Why do you need to know about faculty? Full-time faculty members are most likely to be your mentors. They are the backbone of any department, the people who make curricular and programmatic decisions. They are knowledgeable about the requirements and standards of the program. Learning about their areas of expertise can help you connect with someone who has shared interests, who can guide you through the program and on to graduate school.

- If your school offers *professional counselors,* and you need personal guidance, do not hesitate to use them. Usually these people have degrees in counseling, social work, or clinical psychology. They are professionals who will keep your questions and discussions absolutely private—as a matter of fact, your information must be kept confidential and cannot be accessed by anyone else unless you give signed authorization. Often you will find information about what types of counseling your college offers by going to the student services office, or sometimes a flyer will be posted. No one needs to know that you have called, that you have an appointment, or that you are visiting the counselor on an ongoing basis. Some schools also offer peer counseling, conducted by trained schoolmates.

- Last but not least, speak to your *classmates.* Although you may come up with some misinformation (which should always be double-checked by going to the source), you will at least get a reading of how people have experienced a professor, a course, an exam, or even the library.

Finding a Mentor

Most academics and researchers agree that you should begin a mentoring relationship as soon as possible after you've decided to attend college (Credle and Dean 1991, cited in Freeman 1999). A mentoring relationship can be either formal or informal in nature. In the more formal relationship, a mentor is usually assigned to you. This is often a collegewide procedure and is associated with helping you succeed academically, including helping you stay in college. Your assigned mentor will set up a time to meet and begin the process of getting to know you and what your specific needs may be.

An informal mentor is usually someone you have chosen because you are drawn to something about his or her personality or expertise. The informal relationship serves a more psycho-social function and will have the added dimensions of compatible personalities, shared beliefs, or other characteristics with which you may identify.

Preparing for either a formal or informal mentoring relationship will require that you examine your strengths, weaknesses, beliefs, goals, and the amount of work you are willing to put into the relationship itself. Choosing a mentor assumes that you are an active participant in the construction of your own learning. You are not passively waiting for someone to "discover" you and sweep you off your feet.

To begin the process, look up which courses professors have taught, what their research interests are, and what work they have done in the community. Naturally, the courses that professors teach are listed in the schedule, while their research interests can often be found on the school's web page, or by doing a literature search at the library. You can even Google™ them. If what they have done interests you, take their courses.

Start conversations about subject areas you are interested in. Ask the professor if he or she can give references to other people's work in that area. At the same time, notice how long he or she stays to talk. Ask if you can make an appointment to discuss being mentored. Is the professor responsive? Was he or she a good listener?

When someone agrees to take on this mentoring relationship, prepare for your meetings. If he or she has given you an assignment, do it. Do not return empty-handed. If there was no specific work to be done, create an agenda for the meeting. Two topics should be enough: first, the one that is the most important to you, and then if this is addressed and there's time left, talk about the second item. Meetings shouldn't last more than one hour. Decide together what task you should accomplish before the next meeting.

Access Is a Matter of Knowing the Rules: Skills/Strategies Needed to Gain Access to Mentors

In any organization or institution there must be explicit and tacit agreements made so that the people within the organization can function in an orderly manner. In our society at large we have explicit rules, some of which are known as laws that are written down and, if broken, will result in some kind of punishment. There are also implicit or tacit rules that we follow, which are set up informally but are no less compelling; for example, we participate in and expect particular behaviors during a lecture or the ensuing discussion.

The rules of academic settings are agreements made by the people who govern the university, but also by those who attend it in order to obtain a degree. Historically, the university's "hallowed halls" have been reserved for a select few. Therefore the "rules" that have been developed are not necessarily familiar to everyone. In order to have a successful and fulfilling experience in college, it is in your best interest to uncover the rules and not just follow them but learn how to make them work for you.

These rules include the mandated, clearly articulated, and written expectations of the university that you must fulfill in order to earn your degree. Most of these will be found in the college catalogue, where you can find information about the mission of the institution, administrative policies, fees, students' rights, departmental offerings and requirements, course descriptions, and biographical information about the faculty.

For most Schools of Education within universities, state licensing requirements are written into program requirements. Read these carefully. They are usually easier to interpret than the governing agency's publications, and they are usually more relevant to your immediate situation. The college catalogue is one of the legal documents available to students. It, along with each individual course's syllabus, is a contract between the college and the student. For example, when you take a course, its content should be clearly spelled out in the syllabus and should also be a reflection of the description found in the catalogue. If there is something you don't quite understand, go to someone who does.

Besides the written rules, you will need to become aware of the culture of the organization, in this case, the college or university. The social rules that govern behavior and the academic rules that assess performance may not be clear to you as you begin taking classes. As in any institution, there are hierarchies with some people having more power than others. Herman and Mandell address the issues of power in formal organizations, asserting that they "acquire power with rules, fiscal streams, standardization, efficiency, and the specialization or divisions of expertise and labor" (2004, 31). We have all experienced this in our earlier schooling, especially those of us who went through schools in which we were "tracked" toward particular outcomes, some more academic than others.

Acknowledging these systems, Herman and Mandell (2004) insist that excellent institutions must promote dialogue, and that the rules must be flexible enough so that students as well as faculty feel at ease engaging each other while still remaining autonomous. This flexibility is just as important within the mentoring relationship, so that while your mentor will most likely be more experienced and have higher status within the institution, he or she should be flexible enough to promote an atmosphere of relaxed discourse.

Herman and Mandell (2004) also tackle the subtle notion of *access to* and *access within* the academy, which are closely related to issues of equity and collaboration in the university. Access *to* the academy they argue, is not determined by students' life experiences or practical needs, but rather by the dominant cultural, political, and economic systems of the university, which selects the entering students that meet its standards. And students who succeed will largely reproduce, though in more privileged positions, the same societal values that won them entrance to the university. But access *within* the academy, is governed by different values. The ideal university, being a learning community, should be concerned as much with individual learning as it is with the mechanisms of teaching and furthering knowledge. As such, it should seek to invite, accommodate, and nurture a more genuinely diverse citizenry. A just and equitable learning community depends upon the collaboration—through the exchange of ideas—of all its members, including students. Opening up educational access to the university demands that students and faculty struggle together to address the tension between the elitism of the selection process and the goal of inclusive and collaborative construction of knowledge.

In her seminal work *Other People's Children: Cultural Conflict in the Classroom* (1986), Professor Lisa Delpit addresses what she calls "the culture of power." Delpit argues that in the educational arena, as in other aspects of our culture, those who are successful have been schooled in this culture of power. They are surrounded by the tools of power and are given access to other arenas in which this same culture is replicated. Those who have had less successful school experiences in general, and in the university in particular, are usually not privy to the rules that govern the culture of power, yet are expected to "play" by and be judged by these rules. This has implications for the mentoring experience and your college experience in general, as well as how you deal with issues of power as a teacher. How can you be expected to "play the game" when you don't know the rules? How can you expect the children you teach to "play the game" when they may not know the rules—including rules governing the protocols and procedures necessary to gain access to institutions beyond their community? How will you handle the rules of power once you become a teacher?

Delpit (1986) lists five aspects of power that affect access to education in general and learning in classrooms specifically.

- Issues of power are enacted in classrooms. For example, those who have power outside the institution assume power in classrooms by monopolizing conversations or by expecting to be heard before or to the exclusion of others. This can also happen when someone's authoritative tone is accepted as the only truth.
- There are codes or rules for participating in power; that is, there is a "culture of power." This "culture" excludes members of society who are marginalized in many aspects of American life, including deciding who receives what kinds of education. These rules are not made obvious, although everyone is expected to know them and to participate according to them.
- The rules of the culture of power are a reflection of the rules of the culture of those who have power. In most educational settings, this culture has a long history that suggests that an elite few decide what knowledge is of most worth and who will have access to it.
- If you are not already a participant in the culture of power, being told explicitly the rules of that culture makes acquiring power easier. Delpit argues here that students outside of the culture of power should not be expected to guess at the rules as they gain more and more access to power through schooling. Instructors must make the rules obvious, must teach them to the uninitiated, and must question these rules along the way.
- Those with power are frequently least aware of—or least willing to acknowledge—its existence. Those with less power are often most aware of its existence.

As Delpit points out, those in power are often the last to recognize it. Therefore, you may come across professors and mentors who, in an effort to disguise their power, offer open-ended solutions when you need definitive answers. For example, many early childhood teachers are told to use "developmentally appropriate

Box 3-2

Five rules of power affecting access to education (Delpit 1986)

- Issues of power are enacted in all classrooms.
- There are codes or rules for participating in power, creating a "culture of power."
- The rules of the culture of power reflect the rules of the culture of those who have power.
- Being explicitly told the rules of the culture of power makes acquiring power easier.
- Those with power are frequently least aware of—or least willing to acknowledge—its existence. Those with less power are often most aware of its existence.

practices" (Bredekamp and Copple 1997) with young children. Yet, these practices, such as asking children what they would like to do rather than telling them what they should do, may not fit the cultural approaches familiar to the children in a particular setting. You too may need definitive answers rather than "fishing for meaning."

I am not advocating, and neither is Delpit, that you relinquish what you know and what you bring with you to any learning situation. I am not suggesting that you take on the trappings of the culture of power. As a matter of fact, you must be on your guard not to be enamored of the power you will gain from, for example, having a college degree. The "culture of power" is not omnipotent. It overlooks valuable ways of knowing and the voices of people who have other stories to tell. Adult students often value experiences and knowledge that others bring to the university, and have a deeper understanding of and appreciation for the value of education.

In his article that calls for culturally relevant adult education, Guy (1999, 6) states, "as the numbers of racially, ethnically, and linguistically marginalized learners increase, new approaches to teaching and learning based on the sociocultural experiences and backgrounds of the population must be developed." In other words, not only should you know the rules up front, but the rules themselves must change. If you are not a member of the "culture of power," then, hopefully, being mentored will help guide you through unfamiliar territory. If you are not a member of the "culture of power," then perhaps you will educate your mentor about your need for explicit guidance and support as you negotiate "the rules."

And finally, since the identities and perspectives of many of the children you will teach in publicly funded child care settings and in public schools often come with a sense of "different *and* unequal" (Walkerdine, Lucey, and Melody 2001), hopefully you will consider how educational neglect is replicated. Therefore, in striving for equity in and out of classrooms, you will see the need to "repair . . . deficiencies of the past" (Mancuso-Edwards 1993, 312). By critically examining these children's many debilitating interactions with authority, and by knowing and questioning the rules of the school and the classroom, you will be able to address these discrepancies from an informed position.

Expectations: Yours and Your Mentor's

Both you and your mentor may come to the relationship with differing assumptions, expectations, and needs. These different approaches to mentoring can lead to conflict and can jeopardize the success of your mentored experience. These perspectives may include preconceived notions of what makes a good student, and what good teaching looks like. And, along these lines, you will both have expectations about what each of you should do within the mentoring relationship itself. You may also develop different insights into the ways that both of your needs change as the relationship matures. These perceptions of each other's roles and responsibilities should be made clear from the onset of your relationship so that you can avoid conflicting expectations. Before you meet your mentor, think about these questions.

- What is it that you expect from your mentor?
- To what degree do you expect your mentor to act and interact with you within personal, professional, and social contexts? What would this look like?
- What do you see as your responsibilities?
- How do you see yourself in this relationship?
- What do you hope to gain from the relationship itself?

Then, of course, you must find out what your mentor expects from you. Along with what your mentor considers the characteristics of good mentees, try to uncover what your mentor sees as her responsibilities. How does she envision your work together? What does she consider positive outcomes?

The ability to communicate expectations is going to be something that you both develop as your relationship grows. Practical guidelines regarding commitment, schedules, work load, and availability should be made clear from the start. And just as important, the less tangible aspects of the relationship should be addressed. These may include expecting the mentor to "rescue you" or intervene on your behalf in situations where she may not believe intervention is appropriate. Or you may find yourself disillusioned when your mentor does not "live up to" your ideal expectations. But having opportunities to set up these parameters, and as good educators know, to reflect on interactions that need to be revisited, are always choices.

Characteristics of Good Mentors

This section will help you understand the role played by mentors, so you can seek out, develop, and get satisfaction from good mentored relationships. The more you know about mentors, the easier it is to become a proactive student responsible for your own learning and growth.

The literature on how to mentor can be overwhelming in its scope and volume. There are books on how to mentor in social service fields, such as social work or psychology, how to mentor in business settings, and how to mentor at all levels of education. In education, there are books that teach how to mentor children, adolescents, students at risk of dropping out, adults recovering from trauma, the pre-service teacher, the in-service teacher, the undergraduate, the graduate, and peers or colleagues. The following information is derived from these sources, because if you're looking for a good mentor, you must know what the experts think good mentoring looks like.

A quality mentoring relationship is characterized by mutual comfort and respect, openness to new ideas, and good communication. Equally important is the mentor's expert knowledge, as well as his or her ability to offer encouragement and support, commitment, and time (Heung-Ling 2003).

Prospective mentors are advised to reflect on relationships that work well and to assess what makes these relationships so successful. Before becoming a mentor, they are directed to "consider the traits of your most effective working relationships with other colleagues" (Lee et al. 2006, 233). They are advised to reflect on their teaching skills, management skills, communication skills, and professional ethics. They are told to examine their interpersonal skills in relation to their ability to mentor. In other words, they are advised: *know thyself.*

Mentors are also guided to create a personal statement reflecting their educational philosophy and goals (Lee et al. 2006). Through this statement, they are expected to identify and define how their beliefs shape their philosophy. Mentors are encouraged to communicate openly through verbal and nonverbal cues, notes of encouragement, and to practice effective listening. In our culture, listening is often undervalued and deep listening is a difficult thing to achieve. There are specific ways to listen, to be empathetic, and to stay focused. With these skills, a good mentor will come to know the mentee well, fostering trust, openness, and collaboration.

The mentor is also advised to be the one who plans and organizes your meetings together. It is expected that your mentor has brought up issues in a previous meeting and that the next meeting will start from where you have left off. The mentor of teachers is also advised to arrange meetings with others who are involved in your academic and professional development, such as a cooperating teacher in your student teaching placement. By arranging for this kind of three-way meeting, your mentor is assured that she is modeling proactive and collegial behaviors. By being proactive, your mentor is also modeling professional behaviors.

In terms of problem solving, the mentor is told to identify problems, get to the bottom of things, and to model a calm and positive approach to the investigation and the resolution. Your mentor should focus on the resolution rather than dwell on the problem, and should support your attempts to problem-solve as well.

For Lee and associates (2006) mentors are expected to be reflective practitioners themselves. These authors suggest that mentors keep a diary, prepare questions before meeting with the mentee, and become aware of the potential misuse of authority. I would also suggest that mentors examine their own beliefs and attitudes in relation to their experiences having to do with race, gender, class, and ability, using what Barry Kanpol calls "acts of confession" (Kanpol 1999). Kanpol urges teacher educators to accept, or confess, that they too play a part in "the systematic problems of the world they and their students inhabit" (1999, 72). If mentors are expecting you to use a critical stance in your work with children and families, they should understand that within a mentoring relationship, and "(a)s a necessary condition to becoming critical agents, teacher educators [and mentors] have to begin to use both personal and institutional confession as a part of their daily strategies in order to create the same mindset in their students" (1999, 73). In other words, mentors must first use a critical and reflexive stance in their work with you if that is one of the qualities they hope to develop in the mentoring relationship.

Brad Johnson, a college mentor, and Jennifer Huwe, a graduate student protégé, describe the personality of a good mentor as "characterized by warmth, humor, support, encouragement, flexibility, dedication, patience, and empathy" (2003, 67). The mentor should have a high level of self-awareness, including keeping a healthy balance between work and outside interests. The good mentor models honesty and integrity.

For graduate students, it is important that the mentor be engaged in ongoing and relevant research, and that she or he invites them to join in the process. For under-graduate students, this may seem less important. Yet, being offered opportunities for work beyond the levels expected of you in an undergraduate course, and being able to participate in or observe the organization and methods of a research project, will actu-ally teach you valuable skills as a student and future teacher.

The good mentor is respected by students and his or her peers. The good mentor has had positive and successful mentoring relationships and has a favorable reputation. The good mentor does not gossip. On a pragmatic note, the good mentor is organized, keeps appointments, offers constructive criticism, and engages in ongoing supervision of the mentee. While a missed appointment once in a while is understandable, someone who is habitually late or misses appointments does not consider your time valuable and is giving you a signal that he or she does not take the relationship seriously.

While the characteristics described above seem like a prescriptive application of mentoring, Herman and Mandell (2004), professors at Empire State College, take a more philosophical approach. This program is unique in that it serves working adult students who, with guidance from their mentor, develop an individualized course of study leading to a bachelor's degree. Although Herman and Mandell's book, like most books having to do with mentoring, speak directly to the mentor, what they have to say is useful here too. Using the writings of the philosopher Socrates as a model of mentor-ship, they propose that self-examination and discussion take place in an atmosphere where each other's lived experiences, or what they call "lifeworlds," are welcomed and used as starting frames of reference for further learning.

They call into question what many adults have come to know as "formal educa-tion," proposing instead Dewey's view of experiential learning and Freire's view of shared meaning making as the learner, alongside and in partnership with the teacher, actively constructs knowledge. Herman and Mandell recommend practicing six academic and mentoring principles. In essence, these include the following recommendations.

- To consider that what you know is only conditionally true and that there is always more to learn. This goes back to our understanding of Dewey's reference to "immaturity." If we are always on the lookout for other ways to think about something, we will always be open to learning. For example, working with children and families requires that we always remain open to others' diverse experiences and perspectives.
- To consider that people learn best what they are interested in learning. In early childhood education, we use children's interests to embark on new studies. We call this emergent curriculum.
- To treat all dialogues as occasions for future dialogues and that each participant has something valuable to add. We can refer to Freire here and think about what it means to come together to include more voices and therefore broader definitions.
- To think about all participants in an inquiry as "whole persons" who have experiences that give their lives meaning and purpose. No one is just any one thing: adult students are also workers, family members, or members of

a particular community. In early childhood settings, we develop experiences and assessments that consider the ecological development of the whole child.

- To judge the quality of dialogue and its outcomes like all knowledge: incomplete and diverse. Reflexive communities will serve you well here.
- To honor and engage each individual's desire to know and to value his or her work toward knowing. Good teachers empower learners by pointing out the joys of learning and by sharing the tools with which to learn for a lifetime.

As an early childhood educator I am moved by this list of recommendations. Many of these principles are also found in the characteristics of good early childhood teachers. For example, the notion that learning never ends and that no one person holds all knowledge about any one subject is tied into our use of multiple intelligences, as well as multicultural education and integrated curriculum. Good early childhood teachers offer varied approaches to learning that are meant to meet the needs of diverse learners. You help children learn to find the answers they seek; you do not tell them the answers. You model inquiry and investigation, and develop emergent curriculum by using individual interests. Good early childhood educators open the doors to the many possibilities any one subject can lead to, and you offer countless opportunities to explore them.

The idea that dialogues are enriched by the addition of everyone's voices calls to mind the "morning meeting" in early childhood classrooms. Giving all members of the class opportunities to speak and to add information from their experiences (what Herman and Mandell call "lifeworlds") establishes diverse and rich ways of knowing. And to honor an individual's desire to know and the work he or she does in order to know helps you understand the individual child within the classroom and in the world outside of the classroom. While Herman and Mandell urge the mentor to know the "whole college student," another tenet of early childhood education is to know the "whole child." It would probably be worth your while to think about yourself this way too, looking at how you integrate your social, emotional, academic, physical, cultural, creative, and spiritual worlds.

Looking more closely at these recommendations or principles, the good mentor will always approach knowledge as incomplete and have the attitude that both student and mentor are always learning. For Herman and Mandell, good mentors must *learn* their students, as opposed to evaluating them. In getting to know you, mentors should have an idea of what your responsibilities outside of school are, which courses you are taking, and which are easy and which are difficult. They must recognize and guide you to develop your full potential.

Good mentors will start where you are, scaffolding upon your experiences and expectations. Education of any kind is always contextualized, and, especially within the university, good mentors must be alert to occasions when their own and/or your passive acceptance of "settled" knowledge take over. This type of knowledge is handed down as *the truth* but is really only one component of the countless ways of experiencing this knowledge. The mentor must be aware that in blind acceptance of *the truth,* both of you may become prey to societal definitions of yourselves and others. Modeling critical reflection and sharing meaning with others are also characteristics of a good mentor.

Good mentors also know that optimal learning happens when the learner is connected to or familiar with the thing being studied. Herman and Mandell refer to Dewey's approach to learning and suggest that if mentors "begin with students by honoring and using the immediate contents of their curiosity, they [students] will be all the more likely to happily expand their interests into unfamiliar places" (2004, 28). What is to be learned is driven by the student, as the mentor guides and models inquiry.

Good mentors know that deep-rooted, transformative learning is a result of your active participation as a learner. A good mentor will ask what you want to learn and what you think are your best strengths to help you learn it. Remember that you have already initiated your own intellectual development by coming to college and finding a mentor. Therefore, in order to continue your active participation in your own learning, you may want to ask these questions.

- What are my goals and how will they be met?
- What are the specific components of the work I'll need to do in order to meet these goals?
- What are some ways to organize my work?
- What are some of the most effective ways to reflect on the work while it is in progress?
- How will I revise the work at different stages?
- Once the work is finished, which assessments will I use to identify what I have learned and the processes by which I learned it?

Good mentors listen. They "help their students become autonomous minds fully engaged in the lives they propose to live" (Herman and Mandell 2004, 31). Good mentors also understand that silence can be a valuable and powerful tool. They will, like all good teachers, allow for quiet time as you reflect on an experience, reframe a question to fit your understanding, and formulate new questions to move your work forward. In their silence, mentors are respecting you as a learner, and your ability to formulate your own ideas, ask other questions, and decide upon acceptable solutions.

Good mentors will ask open-ended questions. These kinds of questions will, over time, become so familiar to you that you will take them and shape them into your own questions so that you can continue an internal dialogue about the work at hand. Consequently, you will teach yourself.

Herman and Mandell acknowledge the varied and numerous aspects of lived experience and current demands that adult students bring with them to the university. Therefore, one of their six principles of good mentoring is nurturance. They recommend that "the normal academic expectations of the institution . . . not be taken as ends-in-themselves, but (be) malleable to the students' lifeworlds . . ." (2004, 32). They recommend that mentors within the college understand that adult students will not necessarily adhere to typical time frames and that this should not be confused with one's "intelligence, aptitude, or seriousness of purpose" (2004, 32). The nurturing mentor should contextualize your ability to meet the demands of the program while at the same time support you to successfully adjust to these demands.

Good mentors will collaborate with you to help you develop your learning and professional goals. Therefore, you and your mentor will agree on what it is you want to learn. These outcomes will, and actually should, change along the way. Good mentors will arrange for you to evaluate your own learning (Brookfield 1986) not only in relation to a given professional standard, but in relation to understandings the both of you have defined together over time.

Good mentors will take you seriously and will join with you in the learning process. They will share your curiosity and desire to learn, as midwives in the birthing of new ideas (Belenky et al. 1997). By partnering with you on your journey, they can help you to make connections between your experiences, your inquiry, your explorations, and your discoveries.

Good mentors will wait and help you learn to wait, since in the waiting other facets of an experience may become evident and may lead to more questions, encouraging wonder. "(T)his nurturing of wonder needs only someone to show the cognitive love of paying attention and continuing to ask of each learner, 'Why do you believe this is so? Why do you think this is important? What do you want to learn now?'" (Herman and Mandell 2004, 35). The good mentor asks these questions not just once but over the span of the mentored relationship.

Here I am reminded of the good teacher who values and encourages wonder in young children. Eleanor Duckworth's inspiring book *The Having of Wonderful Ideas & Other Essays on Teaching and Learning* (2006) also comes to mind. While Duckworth instructs teachers on how to nurture children's ideas, she also recommends that adults make time to explore and play with ideas and materials. A good mentor will give you permission to do just that, knowing that from exploration and discovery come true insights.

A mentor should know your individual needs and learning styles. For the good mentor, learning styles are the means by which to foster transformative adult learning. Again, transformative learning occurs when you generate meaning from an experience and reflect on your experiences in order to act upon them effectively (Mezirow 1991).

A good mentor should help you move past simply acknowledging your awareness of an issue to a place where you can clearly and critically evaluate the circumstances of the issue. You may encounter difficulty in accepting and acting upon these new understandings, whether through your own reticence or because of circumstances that are beyond your control. But, by coming to an understanding of your situation, recognizing and naming your feelings, and reviewing your options, you should be able to make more conscientious decisions. An important characteristic of a good mentor is to help you learn how to plan a course of action and to acquire the skills necessary to carry it out (Mezirow 1991).

In the helping relationship model, Gray and Gray (1985) define eight characteristics of the good mentor within teacher education: situational leadership, role model, instructor/promoter of thinking skills, demonstrator teacher, motivator/promoter of realistic values, supervisor, counselor, and promoter of indirect mentoring. They also suggest that you develop relationships with both a primary and a secondary mentor, where the primary one is the closer relationship. Secondary mentors act as supervisors and facilitators within the organization. So, while you may have one mentor who is involved in your academic and personal development, the other mentor may serve to help you stay organized and on task, or be able to get you "through the red tape" of the institution.

Having the above characteristics, a good mentor should help you become a full-fledged member of the academic and social worlds of the university. He or she should be able to bring you into the culture of the particular program while acknowledging, referring back to, and drawing from your "lifeworld" as you move toward your goals. While you may have a friendly and relaxed relationship, it is important to remember that the mentor should be a facilitator, not your "buddy."

The good mentor will provide you with options and not just tell you what to do. She or he may even allow you to struggle and "fail" at some point, most likely at something that is not unalterable. Remember the tasks that Athena set up for Telemachus. The good mentor will guide you, challenge you, help you to learn how to reflect and ask good questions, and apply what you have learned in practical ways.

Mentors often remember their own first experiences that parallel your own. But a good mentor will not present his or her stories so that they become more important than yours. The good mentor will be humble, sharing her struggles and failures as well as her successes and strengths.

Effective mentors therefore have many ways of influencing your undergraduate experience. They will consistently attempt to move you to ever increasing ownership of your project and your own learning.

Characteristics of Good Mentees

As you come to appreciate who you are as a student and therefore who you are as a lifelong learner, you will also come to understand how to make the most of the mentoring relationship. Before you meet with your mentor, try to answer the following questions:

- What are my abilities and strengths?
- To what degree can I accept constructive feedback?
- How do I approach new professional and personal relationships?
- What is my ability to impact the circumstances in my life?
- What is my desire to achieve high academic standards?
- What is my willingness to seek out and develop a mentored relationship?
- What is my plan for academic and professional development?
- Am I able to communicate honestly and directly (assertively, not aggressively)?
- Am I able to tell my mentor how we will both benefit from the relationship?
- To what degree do I depend on others? To what degree do I need their assurance or approval?
- Do I tend to react emotionally to stressful situations?
- Am I able to recognize and respect my personal and professional boundaries and those of others?
- What is my ability to meet deadlines?
- What is my ability to be organized?
  (adapted from Johnson and Huwe 2003, 57)

By writing down your reflections in a journal or notebook, you will be able to refer back to them over time, keep track of your concerns and your strengths, and be aware of your personal and professional growth.

On a more pragmatic note, you should also ask

- What are my goals and objectives? And how will my courses and program requirements help me to meet those goals?
- What obligations do I have outside of school? How will they impact my ability to complete projects or set aside time to study?

- How will my obligations outside school affect my ability to work collaboratively and be committed to meeting with a mentor?
- To what degree am I self-directed and able to take initiative?
- To what lengths will I go to accomplish my goals?

As a good mentee, you will recognize the professional tenor of the relationship. And in doing so, you will realize the limits of your mentor's role and will respect those boundaries. While dropping by once in a while is expected, be conscientious of your own and your mentor's time. Schedule meetings and stick to time limits. Often when everyone realizes there is a finite amount of time to get work done, the work takes precedence and gets done.

While emotional support is something you should expect, it is not the mentor's responsibility to be a psychotherapist. Should you need help with emotional issues, you might breach them with your mentor, but you should seek the help of a professional such as a counselor or therapist. Most universities have a Student Services Office to direct you to the appropriate person for this kind of conference.

While it is important to evaluate your needs and advocate for them, mentors will resist working with a self-absorbed student. As you can imagine, neither you nor your mentor would enjoy working with someone who is unable to compromise, be compassionate, or consider another's needs. While it may be difficult for the student who is so shy that she finds it difficult to clearly articulate what she would like from the relationship, a mentor will expect you to make an effort. Remember, you too are responsible if the relationship is to thrive and succeed.

Prospective mentors are also on the lookout for students who come to the initial meeting unprepared. Don't make this mistake. Before the initial meeting, create a list of topics you would like to cover. Develop a list of questions to ask. Don't be afraid to ask detailed questions. These questions can vary from basic programmatic needs to more philosophical inquiries. For example, asking your mentor about her philosophy of education is an excellent way to know if you will make a good team. Being mentored by someone who does not share your approaches to working with children and families will be difficult. While evaluating your own beliefs as you grow into your role as a teacher is always a good thing, constantly questioning your choices in deference to your mentor's ideals will not help you develop as a teacher in your own right.

When you meet with your mentor, have on hand some way to take notes. Much will be said, and it is almost guaranteed that you will not remember it all. This is especially important when you are in a feedback meeting. Writing down what went well and what you need to work on will be easier to comprehend when you are not so caught up in the conversation. It is the same as reviewing your notes on a child's behaviors—you remember better with just a few short phrases, when you are not so emotionally involved, and by reflecting-on-action where you can often see more clearly what to do next.

Again, don't underestimate what you bring to the relationship. As an adult you have had many experiences that will enrich your education and lend you credibility as a teacher. Your work with a mentor is to develop your own sense of self, not to become the mentor's clone. M. J. McAuley (2003) cautions against what she calls "transference and coutertransference in the mentor-mentee relationship" (14). While you may find yourself in awe of your mentor's accomplishments and must respect his or her expertise, you should be careful that you do not lose who you are in the relationship. Stay true to your goals while allowing these goals to develop.

As an adult learner actively engaged in your own learning, you will be expected to work with your mentor to set your own goals, define the process by which you can attain those goals, be accountable for your own growth, see your work through to completion, and assess the entire process once your work has been accomplished.

Successful Mentoring Relationships

Since the program at Empire State College offers such a clear model of formal mentoring, A. M. Langer (2001) studied their faculty to understand how they actually practice mentoring. While professors and instructors reported that they were free to develop their own approaches to mentoring, many also reported that they incorporated mentoring models from management and business. They felt that since they were working with adults, most of whom were employed, it would be best to set academic goals that took workplace relationships into consideration. The faculty reported being very much in touch with the needs of their adult students and took a transformational approach to teaching. They described allowing students to define their own learning goals, within a "practical and hierarchical mode to help students complete their course requirements" (54). In other words, while the faculty believed that the learner should lead the investigation of the subject at hand, they felt it was important to organize the work, hold on to their status, and be in a position to evaluate the student's performance.

Faculty mentors also reported that one of their key functions was to develop a strong relationship with their mentees. Using a transactional approach to learning (Cohen 1995; Daloz 1999; Galbraith 1991; cited in Langer 2001), these faculty members held regularly scheduled meetings with their mentees where both members of the relationship could actively benefit from exchanging information. They described receiving great satisfaction when their student-oriented approach helped "integrate academic activities with a student's particular interests and goals, to make education as relevant as possible to the student's needs" (Langer 2001, 55).

In a successful mentoring relationship both you and the mentor will acknowledge that there are stages in the process of being mentored. A good mentor will help you through the stages of the relationship. According to Chip Bell (2000), who writes about mentoring from a corporate perspective, mentoring is a partnership. In a successful mentoring partnership you and your mentor are both learners. The relationship between you must be safe, balanced, and a place where each of you can advocate for yourself and for each other.

Bell writes that a mentoring partnership will go through four stages. The first is what he calls "leveling the learning field" (2000, 54). Your mentor should create an environment where you can experience true partnership and "rapport"—a word that Bell points out comes from French and means "connection renewed." Rapport will occur when you do not fear reprisal or embarrassment and feel safe enough to take risks, ask questions, and examine your work together.

The second stage also contributes to the character of the relationship and gets you ready to be able to hear and accept your mentor's ideas. Your mentor should not appear to be testing or judging you. By the time you reach this stage, you will have become accustomed to the fact that your mentor is not just listening, but that she values what you are saying. Bell asserts, and I agree, that when you feel valued, you will be more likely to take risks and envision new ways to approach learning.

For Bell, you must go through the first two steps in preparation for the third, receiving "learning gifts" (2000, 55). For Bell, mentors give many gifts: advice, feedback, support, focus, courage, and affirmation, to name a few. Bell asserts that in a trusting partnership, you will accept guidance as part of the process and should any challenges arise, they are the mentor's responsibility to untangle.

Finally, Bell addresses what happens when the mentoring relationship comes to a close. He says that these endings are bittersweet since you and your mentor will miss each other's company. Yet both of you will reach a point where you consider the inevitable step of separation as a healthy and necessary development in your professional and personal growth. The healthiest mentoring relationships will have gotten you ready for future mentoring relationships, including ones where you become the mentor.

If we were to go back to Dewey's position on learning through experience, the mentored relationship can be thought of as an experience in and of itself, aside from the content knowledge that you aspire to learn. And, coming from a constructivist approach, it is advisable that you be conscious that the mentor's role is to support you without taking over or attempting to "rescue" you. The mentor should provide you with many opportunities for experiential learning, scaffolding these experiences so that you are able to tackle increasingly difficult tasks. Therefore you will learn while experiencing, through trial and error, by observing a more experienced person, or by direct guidance (Kerka 1998). The mentor will assist you as you form your own ideas, making your knowledge and understanding known. In formulating these ideas, missteps will occur—either in your own attempts to define the idea or in the way the mentor understands what you are saying. This is not necessarily a bad thing.

As we know from our work with young children, making mistakes is inevitable and actually desirable in any learning situation. Making mistakes helps us see how we are thinking about a problem. Mistakes are opportunities for learning about divergent ways to approach an issue. Great ideas come from understanding what you would have liked to see happen as well as examining what actually occurred. If we consider making mistakes as opportunities that open out onto different ways of thinking, then the ability to explore and experiment could become important and salient aspects of the experience of being mentored.

In their book *The Good Teacher Mentor* (2003), Sidney Trubowitz (an education professor emeritus and mentor) and Maureen Picard Robbins (a first-year teacher and mentee) discuss how aspects of their yearlong successful mentoring relationship challenged and supported their understandings and practices of teaching and mentoring. Both authors describe their own experiences in terms of the roles they played in the relationship, in the university, and in the school system in which Maureen worked. It is an excellent reference for new teachers who are lucky enough to have a mentor as they take on this role. Most importantly, both Trubowitz and Robbins offer helpful insights into what a thriving relationship might look like. For example, when Maureen speaks about a small accomplishment her mentor helped her see, she asserts that she "enjoyed the perspective of an outsider sharing with me new ways to consider a particular event" (107). She also talks about how grateful she was for his guidance as he steered her away from teachers who "saw the children as lost causes . . . [and] the . . . veteran instructors who pass down a culture of indifference" (107). Mostly, Maureen learned to see her own teaching "as a workable, changeable thing . . . [that] the negotiation between the demands of the system and what keeps me excited as a learner . . . will shape my teaching voice" (107).

In this book, Maureen offers a list of dos and don'ts for mentors and mentees alike. While she addresses mentors directly with ideas like "listen to mentees and transform their ideas into workable lessons, not lessons *you* create and want to see taught," her suggestions for mentees are most helpful. To you she says

- *Don't* take offense if your mentor jumps in. Mentors don't mean to be offensive, just proactive. They may be over enthusiastic or miss being in their own classrooms.
- *Do* keep an eye out for another person on the staff who might be a natural mentor for you.
- *Don't* get frustrated if your specialty is language arts and you are matched with the retired science teacher. While mentors from other subject areas may have little to offer in the way of content area expertise, they might have some keen ideas about skill building or classroom management. (This may be different for early childhood educators who would do best with someone who understands the differences in pedagogy and philosophies of working with young children as opposed to just a difference in content knowledge.)
- *Do* figure out what your mentor has to offer and take it all.
- *Do* "kid watch" when your mentor models a lesson. Monitoring kid reaction will help you refine the approach you see in a way you feel is more useful.
- *Do* use video and audio tape-recording equipment in order to revisit classroom activities and learn from what you see and hear.
- *Do* keep a log. Your thoughts and what you discussed with your mentor provide much material for you to consider.
- *Do* listen. Make eye contact, sit knee to knee, and be ready to respond to what your mentor is saying. (2003, Appendix C, 119)

Finally, when working with a mentor, you should always keep in mind that "if their accounts [of an event] turn out to be different, there is . . . no reason for assuming that the content of only one [perspective] . . . can be real and the experiences of the others must necessarily be any less accurate or real" (Biesta and Burbules 2003, 43). By being reflective and participating in reflexive settings, you will certainly understand and take into account that the ways *you* respond to others' actions, and the meanings *you* attribute to *their* actions, will impact on your mentoring relationship. You will also easily understand that a truly successful mentoring relationship develops over time, while you and your mentor adjust accordingly.

Working with Specific Kinds of Mentors

An overview of the different types of mentors and supports that teacher education candidates will encounter

❖ Working with a Professor

❖ Student Teaching and Your Cooperating Teacher

❖ Student Teaching, Your Field Supervisor, and Clinical Supervision

❖ On the Job: Directors or Principals, Colleagues, and Consultants

❖ Social Supports: Family, Friends, and Fellow Students

❖ Being Assertive: Getting What You Need Using DERM

Whatever type of mentoring relationship you cultivate, in order for you to benefit from it, you should feel comfortable, have respect for the mentor and feel respected in turn, have frequent and open communication, and sense that the mentor is committed to your success. According to Gray and Gray (1985), effective mentors will be interested in your ideas, like working with you, and will help build your confidence as you work toward your goals.

In a perfect world, your mentor will approach the relationship from a holistic framework, much the same as we do in early childhood classrooms, looking at cultural/ social, emotional, cognitive, physical, creative, and spiritual facets of the whole child's development. As Martin and Trueax (1997) point out, mentors of early childhood educators will be cognizant of adult and child development, will reference developmentally and culturally appropriate practices for young children as well as adults, will expect you to be a reflective practitioner as well as reflect on their own practices, and will follow the guidelines of developmental supervision.

Working with a Professor

In undergraduate teacher education settings, your mentor will most likely be one of your professors. This person may be assigned to mentor you, or at least supervise you during your student teaching semester. This professor may be someone you have become close to over the course of your undergraduate experience. Maybe you enjoyed her course and you sought her out, asking her to mentor you. Perhaps this person changed your way of looking at teaching as a profession or changed the way you look at your own learning.

The spirit of mentoring can be found in the quality of the relationship. In my own experience as a student, I found that I would be attracted to one particular professor within my program or that someone had stepped up coming to my aid when I needed her, and a mentoring relationship developed from there. However we connected, this became my primary mentoring relationship (Gray and Gray 1985). This person fulfilled the role of a classic mentor by taking an interest in my academic development and my personal and professional growth. She willingly shared her expertise with me and often opened doors to opportunities that I never would have had without her.

According to Campbell and Campbell (2000), most students in a mentoring program are interested in getting help with academic issues. Naturally, you will most likely turn to one of your professors to fill this role. As you begin, you and your mentor will plan what work you want to accomplish. This can be anything from improving writing skills to learning how to access and interpret research on the Internet. The plan should not only consist of *what* you want to do, but *how* you want to do it.

Make sure that you both have the same goals in mind when you begin. Be clear about your needs. Repeat what you have agreed to, making sure that you have heard what was said and not what you may have wanted to hear.

The next step is to carry out the assignment or task. If your work is focused on research and writing, and you have no experience doing this, it may be best for you to plan a session with your mentor in which you can actually write or use a computer together. On the other hand, the mentor may feel that this is not part of her definition of mentoring. She may instead send you to work with a writing tutor or to the computer lab to do this part of the assignment, checking in with you periodically, and responding only to the work you hand in. As part of your work together, you should discuss whether written assignments can be done in stages. Writing drafts is an important technique to learn.

Your mentor should read your work, acknowledging that it is a draft, and give you feedback on it. For your next meeting together, you should both sit and review the comments and corrections made, again asking for clarification when needed. It may be helpful for you to take notes during the conference. This scaffolding approach should help you recognize your strengths as a writer and the patterns of errors you make in your writing.

You should leave this conference with an understanding of what you did that is acceptable, what you did that needs improvement, and what you still need to do. At this point, you should make a plan together for what work needs to be accomplished before the next conference. Again, repeat what you think you both have agreed to do. Then do it.

The ideal mentoring relationship would have your professor, your mentor, and your field supervisor all be the same person. This would encourage a more holistic understanding of your growth as a teacher. In this case, the professor/mentor/supervisor will have firsthand knowledge of your student-teaching placement, the cooperating teacher, and, of course, your performance.

If this is not the case—for example, you have someone other than your mentor supervising you in the field—then you must make sure your mentor has a clear understanding of your placement and your work.

Most often the mentor will make an effort to either visit your site or have an ongoing relationship with your field supervisor. He or she will naturally discuss your progress or any issues that may arise. If you have any concerns, or are having difficulties with any one of the components of your student teaching experience, try to bring your mentor and the field supervisor together for a three-way meeting. Much like the three-way conference that might take place with your field supervisor, your cooperating teacher, and you, this type of meeting can be invaluable in clarifying any questions any one of you may have, or in resolving any conflicts that may develop.

While your professor/mentor will most likely have the most influence, the three of you have one thing in common: your academic and professional growth. Just as you prepared for your writing conference, be organized for this meeting too. Know the agenda, take notes, clarify issues, and plan what to do next.

Remember, the supports you receive during this time will unfortunately come to an end, so what you get from these interactions should actually go beyond the moment or the isolated issue. Being aware of the nuances of being mentored will help you develop more than just immediate solutions, but also the frameworks that will serve you well during your entire career.

Student Teaching and Your Cooperating Teacher

Besides being mentored within the college environment, you will also be working with teachers in their classrooms. These cooperating teachers often have an ongoing relationship with the college supervisor or the field placement officer. For most students, the cooperating teacher will become a new mentor. While you may not meet the cooperating teacher until the day you arrive in her classroom and begin your student-teaching placement, your relationship can become one of the most important aspects of your learning to teach. And, since this is such an important relationship where you will be mentored "on the job" before you are contractually responsible for a classroom full of children, you should not take this relationship for granted. Often, your relationship will have to develop within a short period of time—sometimes in one semester or less. Therefore, you should make the most of every opportunity to learn in it and to get what you need from it.

You should not expect nor be expected to "jump right into" the life of the classroom. The culture of the school and the tone of the class will be unfamiliar to you. The cooperating teacher's philosophical approaches to teaching and learning will unfold over time. Depending on when you start your student teaching placement, fall or spring semester, the relationships among the children as well as their relationships with the teachers will also become evident over time. If you begin in September, when everyone else is starting the school year, you will be a "taken for granted" member of the class. If you begin your student teaching during the spring semester, you will have to observe relationships and routines that have already developed. While most children accept new people into their classrooms in stride, you will have to learn what everyone else takes for granted. Give yourself time to do this.

If you consider your position in the classroom together with what you have observed of the classroom setting—for example, is it organized or chaotic, is there a clear schedule or are time limits ignored and children often rushed to the next activity—you will get a sense of the teacher's strengths and weaknesses not only in working with children but in her ability to mentor adults.

Most cooperating teachers are happy to have you in their classrooms. They are usually asked if they want a student teacher in their room and are often given the right to decline having one. Therefore, if you are in someone else's classroom, she most likely asked to have a student teacher that semester. Not only do teachers want someone in the room to help them work with the children, but they see themselves as capable and interested in mentoring a new teacher. Still, it is important to remember that not all teachers are taught to supervise or work with adults. Even those teachers who are gifted in working with children may not be able to transfer those skills to working with another adult.

Cooperating teachers are often given guidelines regarding their responsibilities by the college's student teaching placement office. These guidelines are part of a professional agreement. It may help you to go over these guidelines with your cooperating teacher, making clear what your roles and responsibilities are in this classroom and what his or her responsibilities are to you and to the college.

The cooperating teacher is expected to welcome you into the life of the classroom. He or she should offer you many opportunities to work with children. You should have one-on-one interactions with each child. You should lead the whole group: for example, conduct the morning meeting or read a story. You should write observations and the two of you should discuss what you learn from these records and your opinions about particular children. You should be encouraged to plan and contribute ideas for curriculum development. You should be able to carry out particular experiences with small groups of children, and you should expect to be able to revisit these in order to hone your craft.

Malcolm

Malcolm had never been in an early childhood classroom before his student teaching placement. He was excited to finally get started using all the things he learned in his courses. He arrived early on the first day of his placement and stayed late, helping the cooperating teacher organize materials and children's work.

As Malcolm grew familiar with the children, the schedule, and the tone of this kindergarten class in a public school, he grew concerned about some of the cooperating teacher's management skills. He expressed this to his peers during the student-teaching seminar:

"The kids are out of control. There's no discipline. They're allowed to get up and walk around during meetings, and there's one girl who immediately cries whenever she doesn't get what she wants. I mean, it's February already! Shouldn't this have been taken care of awhile ago? It seems like this teacher needs these kids to rely on her for everything. And at the same time, they're showing her that they don't really need her, since they seem to decide to do what they want anyhow. How do I tell her that she shouldn't be letting these kids get up at meetings? I mean, if I ever treated my elders like that, I'd have gotten my behind whacked! This teacher needs some help, but I'm not being paid to supervise her!"

- What kinds of information would you need to know more about if you were to offer to help Malcolm?
- Thinking about the tone of Malcolm's telling of this story, how might you help him broaden his perspective?
- What steps, if any, would you suggest he take to resolve this dilemma?

During the seminar's next weekly meeting, Malcolm reported:

"YES! Today I had them by myself for the meeting. The teacher was grading the reading test they had taken the day before. She was sitting at the back of the room and let me lead the meeting. Well, Zachary starts to get up to take his usual walk around the room while we have a group discussion. I just couldn't let that happen anymore. I told him he could come sit by me or he could sit back in his place, but that he couldn't walk around, not when I'm leading the group. I used that low, slow voice we've talked about—that kids really hear. Well, he stopped in his tracks, looked at me, didn't say a word, and came and sat right next to me! I was shocked but I felt so good. I told him I knew he could make the right choice. I felt so good that I could set limits. Zach actually listened to other kids and joined in the conversation, adding some really good ideas. And after the meeting I went over to him again and praised him, telling him that I thought the other kids were really interested in his ideas.

Now all I want to know is, what do I do so all my work doesn't get undone?"

- In what ways do you think Malcolm is using reflection-on-action?
- To what degree do you think Malcolm's last question is answerable?
- Describe a situation where you may have seen the need for change but were not in a position of power to make it happen. What did you do?

You and your cooperating teacher should meet regularly, at a scheduled time. You should receive feedback after an experience, and immediate guidance if necessary when things aren't going as planned. You and your cooperating teacher have a nonspoken agreement to support each other's lifelong learning—yours as a novice teacher, hers as a leader and mentor to others in the profession.

Your relationship with the cooperating teacher/mentor will be influenced not only by the university's guidelines, but also by your college supervisor's participation. As well as the cooperating teacher having a say in whether or not she would like a student teacher to work in her classroom, the college supervisor's job is to have observed this teacher and assessed her ability to work with children. Although the college supervisor relies on the center's director or the school's principal to recommend classroom teachers to mentor students, the supervisor should also have a say in who you will work with. Therefore, you should assume that the cooperating teacher to whom you are assigned will be ready, willing, and able to mentor you during your stay in her class.

The following are some of the protocols for beginning student teaching in someone else's classroom.

Arrive early. By being early you are showing that you are eager to learn all that is offered. You will also become familiar with the ways in which the cooperating teacher prepares the environment for the children and plans for the activities of the day.

Stay late. By staying late you are showing that you take your placement seriously and you are approaching this experience professionally. Great teachers often spend time in the classroom before and after the children have been there. They set up, clean up, and prepare for the next day as part of their workday.

Observe. As you do with children, you will learn the cooperating teacher's methods, pace, and tone by insightful watching. A good mentor will understand your need to spend at least the first day watching what happens in the classroom.

Take notes. As you observe, record what you see. Work out a system where you can make notations about what you see, for example, using the margins to ask yourself questions about what is happening, things you may disagree with, or ideas for follow-up

Box 4-1

Student teaching in someone else's classroom:

Arrive early.	Stay late.
Observe.	Take notes.
Use a journal.	Volunteer often.
Plan.	Collaborate.
Follow through.	Get feedback.

experiences you might want to offer the children. You might also be able to photograph areas of the classroom or charts and graphs that you find especially appealing or useful.

Use a journal. Journaling is also a great way to revisit what has happened in the classroom on any given day. Get in the habit of reflecting-on-action at the end of the day: what happened, what particular children did, what the cooperating teacher did, what you did, what was done that was successful, or what could have been done differently.

Volunteer often. This also shows your eagerness to learn and gives you opportunities for hands-on learning. It is not necessary to test yourself with activities that are unfamiliar. You will want to volunteer for roles where you can be successful at first. If you scaffold your responsibilities and your work with children, it will be easier to take on more and more difficult tasks. Usually this means working one-on-one with a child, then with a small group, then with the whole class. Using the children's familiarity with material or a routine will help you carry out a successful activity.

Plan. You must make your cooperating teacher aware of your plans to work with children in specific areas. If you plan an activity and the cooperating teacher is unaware of your intentions, she may not leave time for your work or she may have other work in mind for you to do.

Collaborate. By presenting and discussing your ideas and your plans, the cooperating teacher will be in a better position to know how to guide you in your interactions with children. Notice that I have placed collaboration after planning. I believe that this will help you to think about your work on your own first, then in presenting it to the cooperating teacher, you and she can revisit your plans and work together to hone them, make them all the more doable, and be sure they relate to the curriculum at hand.

Follow through. If you say you will take responsibility for something, do it. Do it on time. Give it your all. Being responsible and trustworthy lays the foundation for the cooperating teacher to trust that you can carry out assignments with children on your own. These seemingly simple traits will serve to open doors that give you access to more and more demanding teaching roles.

Get feedback. You and the cooperating teacher should have at least one scheduled conference a week. It would be best if this time was mutually agreed upon and that it became part of your weekly schedule. Besides having a formal conference in which you both examine your performance and growth, you should expect informal conversations that let you know how you're doing.

Your ability to be open to instruction, reflect on what worked and what didn't work and why, and apply these lessons to other situations will set the stage for transformative learning.

Student Teaching, Your Field Supervisor, and Clinical Supervision

If your supervisor is not your professor, most likely he or she is someone who has been hired by the college to supervise student teachers in the field. It is safe to assume that your field supervisor has many years of experience in early childhood settings. Often retired teachers or directors will do this work. Having reached a master level of professional development, most field supervisors are happy to participate in classrooms with young children and to have input in the development of new teachers.

Your supervisor most likely will have been trained by the college or the early childhood faculty in the methods of supervision used by the department. Sometimes your field supervisor will also lead a seminar or advisory group for student teachers. These groups serve to support you in your student teaching experience and are often led as a seminar where the topics to be discussed are developed by the instructor and students together. Usually the topics reflect what is happening in your own or your peers' placements. It has been my experience that these seminar cohorts often develop into ongoing support groups. Graduates stay in contact and support each other during their first years in their own classrooms.

Even though your supervisor may not be involved in your academic work, he or she may be willing to help you with it. Part of having developed a trusting relationship is knowing that you can ask your supervisor for different types of guidance and feedback.

It is important to understand from the outset that supervision is not evaluation, just as testing is not assessment. Being supervised during your hands-on experience in a classroom is just one aspect of being supported as a new teacher. As I tell my students, a good supervisor is going to watch you work with children more than once, looking for your strengths and the gaps in your knowledge or practice. A good supervisor will not bring along a checklist of what every teacher should know and do. I don't think one even exists. Certainly your supervisor will not be expecting a perfect performance, and, in early childhood classrooms, may not even be expecting a formal "lesson."

So then, what *is* supervision and why are you subject to it? And what does it have to do with being mentored?

Just as there are many models and guides about how to mentor, there are many books on how to supervise. Unfortunately, most people think of supervision as an adversarial interaction between managers and workers. In school settings, this model was used when "inspectors" came into the school to ensure that standards were being met. This happens today in day care and other public child care settings when health and safety or governing agencies visit for licensing renewal inspections. Often, the person who is doing the evaluation has little or no interaction with the classroom teachers or the children and is not involved with the center in an ongoing relationship. Supervision, on the other hand, is much like the assessment you will do of children, requires observations, reflections, dialogues, planning, awareness of growth over time, and a partnership focused on your development.

Although the word *clinical* can bring to mind the medical, scientific, or even detached or dispassionate interactions in teacher education, this kind of supervision is actually framed by a humanistic teacher-centered approach. Goldhammer uses the term *clinical* to mean "(C)lose observation, detailed observational data, face-to-face interaction between the supervisor and teacher, and an intensity of focus that binds the two together in an intimate professional relationship" (1969, cited in Acheson and Gall 1997, 54). In teacher preparation programs, clinical supervision most often takes place during student teaching. It is comprised of a sequential cycle of events that include preparation, observation, analysis, feedback, examination of the supervision itself, and, if all parties find the supervision acceptable, preparation for the next meeting (Hyun and Marshall 1997).

Clinical supervision is one of the most effective methods your mentor can use to guide you, especially since you will both be examining and assessing your work. This kind of supervision, like the mentored relationship in general, requires your active participation. Since the main objective of clinical supervision is professional development, and a key to professional development is the ability to reflect-on-action, or develop and refine reflective practice, your voice must be part of the process. The goal of this supervisory model is to instill elements of reflective practice as part of your repertoire of academic and teaching performance. Like good mentoring, good supervision should strengthen your motivation, your classroom practices, and your ability to reflect on your own work.

The clinical supervision model is made up of three phases. The first is the *planning conference.* During this time, you and your mentor/supervisor will meet to discuss your goals for a particular cycle. This is usually defined in broad terms, but can be more specific. For example, you may think that classroom management is the big concern, but the transition from lunch to rest time may turn out to be the particular issue.

During this planning meeting, you and your supervisor can review the experience you have planned to do with the children. You should discuss the plan for that specific observation: the activity, the materials needed, time of day that it will take place, and

Box 4-2

Questions to consider before being observed:

- Do I want to try something I have never done before with young children?
- Is it an activity the children have never experienced in this classroom?
- Will the cooperating teacher let me "practice" before my supervisor comes?
- Is it an experience that I have done with children before, but want to learn more about the way I carry it out?
- For example, should I ask that my supervisor focus on one particular aspect of my teaching, how I modulate my voice while I read a story?
- What is it that I want to learn about my own teaching?

Box 4-3

Example of a written outline to help you prepare and organize the planned experience:

- Where the observation will take place
- What materials will be needed; what research you may have to do beforehand
- How many children can work together at this activity
- Steps you will take to introduce the materials and ideas
- Questions you may want to ask
- Learning goals you have for the children
- Specific aspects of your performance that you may want the supervisor to especially notice

what type of data collection would be helpful. For example, would it be more helpful to have your supervisor keep running records as she observes, or would you rather that she take a video recording of you in action?

I do not call these written formats "lesson plans." I believe that in early childhood classrooms, children learn from experiences, not lessons in the didactic sense of the word. While you may offer the materials and the setting for an experience, trying to imitate a traditional teacher-directed "lesson" will most likely leave you frustrated. Part of what is so wonderful about teaching young children is that you never really know what their responses will be. Preparing open-ended, inquiry-based questions would be a better use of a written plan.

The second phase of the supervisory cycle is the actual *observation.* Again, this is not a surprise visit but happens at an agreed-upon time and place, and focuses on an activity or interaction that you would like to assess. The supervisor will arrive and sit unobtrusively in the classroom, taking notes on what she sees. Most often supervisors will not interfere. When the observation is complete, she may stay and talk with you or the cooperating teacher for a while, or may leave, having set a time for the next meeting.

The third phase is the *feedback conference.* This takes place after all of the above have been accomplished. This feedback session is a continuation of conversations—and the planning conference in particular—that you and your mentor/supervisor have had previously. Its function is to give an accurate representation of what occurred in the classroom during the observation itself.

In preparation for this part of the supervisory cycle, you should write a reflection of the experience that the supervisor observed. Reflecting-on-action is an important part of learning to become a teacher. Coming to a feedback conference just to hear what someone else thinks will not help you learn to review your own work when that someone else is no longer available.

Again, these should be written reflections so that you don't forget anything during the feedback conference.

I also believe that *you* should begin the feedback conference. This allows you to reflect and report on your own inferences and feelings about what you did without being swayed by someone else's ideas or opinions. In this way you practice reflection

Box 4-4

Post-observation reflection:

- How did I prepare for the experience? Was there anything more I could have done?
- How did I introduce the experience to the children? How do I know if they understood?
- What happened that went well?
- What happened that didn't go so well?
- What happened that was unexpected? What did I do? What does that tell me about myself?
- What kinds of questions did I ask? Why did I think it was necessary to ask those questions?
- Did I redirect the discussion so that children spoke to children? How?
- Did I feel comfortable with the pace? Did the children?
- How did I bring the experience to a close?
- What would I do again? What would I leave out or change? Why?
- In what ways am I satisfied with what happened?
- Ideas for a follow-up experience or ways that I might repeat this experience.

itself as the supervisor responds to the things you mention, and this can help you hone your skills for reflection-in-action and reflection-on-action.

The observer has her notes and has organized them so that you both can go through them and analyze what she saw. Her report to you should be objective. Since no data collection can be completely objective, her report should be free of assumptions or judgments, much like the observation and recording techniques teachers use to gather information about children's behaviors. As a good mentor, her observation should be descriptive, including feedback on the specific things you asked her to observe.

The mentor/supervisor's written notes should describe what you were doing, what the children were doing, and perhaps even incidents that were taking place throughout the classroom. Her notes should include examples of your exact words and should address your use of language and vocabulary as well as your factual knowledge. She should describe the explanations you used, and what you did if a child didn't understand. She should also point out instances where you reflected-in-action, changed your approach, or corrected yourself. For example, there may be notes on how you responded when a child asked a question that you didn't know the answer to. Or, as another example, what you did when ten children ran to the cooking table and you had only planned for four.

The observer might have recorded data that focus on one aspect of your teaching, such as what you said to children. While you may have wanted her to note how you integrated science and math during the experience, recording what you said can be a way to focus on your ability to foster content-specific inquiry with appropriate questions.

There will also be information about and descriptions of specific things that will need to be improved. That is expected. Good teaching thrives on improvement through reflection. A good mentor will have a nonthreatening manner, using descriptive language and fact-based data. She should ask open-ended questions that lead you to think about what took place. A good mentor will "walk you through" the data, helping you to see where there are opportunities for improvement. And, since the two of you are working together, your insights may in fact point to items the observer did not see.

By having analyzed and interpreted the objective data of your performance, you are ready to plan for the next experience you will offer children. Remember to use a written format that is most helpful to *you*. This format in itself may be something to discuss with your supervisor. Does it meet your needs? Where did it originate? Is it written from an early childhood educator's perspective; for example, does it refer to children as "children" and not as "students"? Is it focused on experiential understandings or content knowledge?

When you plan the next experience, take into consideration what you have just learned from your own written reflection and from the feedback conference. Think about behaviors, good and not so good, that may have been pointed out to you and that you weren't previously aware of. Visualize yourself doing the activity with children as you write the next plan. Then decide: do I want to revisit the same experience and compare the data for each, or do I want to examine another aspect of my teaching style? While you will probably not come away from the feedback conference with the entire planned experience written up, you and your supervisor should have a good idea of what you will do, where you will do it, when, and what you want her to note in particular, repeating phase one. Schedule the next observation.

And there we have the cycle of clinical supervision.

How does this relate to being mentored? Well, the clinical supervision model is an excellent model for being mentored in any field. The ability to plan, experience, and reflect on your work is the goal of all good mentoring. Remember, you want to be able to do these things when you are no longer being mentored. Should you find yourself being mentored in another setting, you can bring these skills to the relationship. And, when you become the more experienced person—for example, taking a student teacher into *your* classroom—you will have the foundation for a productive relationship.

Mary

Mary had emigrated to the United States from Ireland soon after graduating from high school. She worked as a sous-chef but gladly gave that up when she married. She became a stay-at-home mom, devoting herself to her two children. When her youngest son was ready to start fifth grade, Mary decided she was ready to go back to work. She had always been interested in working with young children and thought that teaching would be a perfect match for her young family's schedule. Mary enrolled in the early childhood program and was an A student. She was conscientious and curious. She often went beyond the course assignments, sometimes doing research on a topic that interested her. She delighted in the philosophies she read about in early childhood education, and found that they were worlds apart from her own parochial education. She sailed through the program and couldn't wait to get into a classroom.

"Only thing is, I have no experience with young children in a school setting. I mean, I have kids of my own, but I never took charge of someone else's children."

Mary was assigned to work in a second grade classroom in a public school. Her cooperating teacher was considered a master, and her supervision of children as well as adults allowed everyone great leeway to follow up on questions and explore interests. This was an ideal setting for Mary and she said, "I think the way Justine runs her classroom is the way I see myself running a classroom. I like the way the kids know what's expected of them, yet they can feel like what they discover is really their own doing."

For the first formal observation, Mary planned to carry out a math lesson. When I arrived, she was working with six children at a corner table. It was clear from the start that two of the children were having difficulty with the work and had begun to distract each other, jabbing each other and rocking on their chairs. Mary was concentrating on getting them back to their worksheets while at the same time trying to ask the other children questions to see what they understood about the work. Mary began to bombard the children with questions, one after the other, often not waiting for answers. Her face became red with effort as she looked from me to the children and back to me again. I whispered, "It's OK. I'm here to help, not to give you a grade." She relaxed a bit and finished the lesson without really getting the two boys who had lost interest back to their work.

When we met for our reflective conference, I asked Mary what she thought about what I had seen. She said, "Well, it was pretty bad, wasn't it?" She waited for me to respond, but I told her to keep going with her reflection. "I wanted the kids to learn about grouping so I had them draw circles around sets of five objects on the page. Some of the kids got it really easily, but some were having trouble. And those two boys . . . they're always getting each other going. I wish I had something else for them to do. I felt like I couldn't handle everything at once. But I think most of the children understood."

I asked Mary to think about the physical set up of the lesson: six children at a table and where each child sat. She laughed and said, "Yeah, I thought of that . . . I should have had those boys separated. And maybe six kids were too many at once." I asked if there were any manipulatives the children could have used instead of just working on paper. "We have unifix cubes. I guess we could have used those. But the cooperating teacher wants them to learn this in a more abstract way." I wondered, "What about the children who were having trouble with the work? How could you have helped them?" Mary answered, "Well, I kept asking them questions to find out what they understood, but then I lost control of the rest of them." I asked Mary if she thought about her questions and the ways she posed them. She said, "Well, I knew you were watching and I got worried that I wasn't teaching them . . . and then I started to ask questions but no one answered." I asked Mary to try to think back to the lesson and imagine hearing herself, "If the kids weren't answering, what does that tell you? Try to get your cues from the children." Mary thought a moment and said, "I guess I spoke too much. I knew it was bad, but now I think it was truly awful." I reassured her that the children would survive and that she was also there to learn. We spoke about what happens when you are busy asking too many questions. "It's funny; I didn't realize I was talking so much. But I see what you mean; the children didn't answer me because these weren't even real questions, they were more about my being nervous than about their learning."

When I visited Mary next, she had indeed taken a cue from the children. They had started a unit on the solar system, and Mary was working with a group who were making "postcards from another planet." They chose their planet and researched facts about it, drew a picture of it, and wrote about it to someone. Mary had brought in a small replica of the solar system and the children enjoyed rotating the planets around the sun. All the children were deeply engaged in this work, and Mary walked around the table checking in with each child. She stopped at one little girl and stayed with her as they sounded out words and the child wrote what she heard. One child decided to make a book instead of a postcard and Mary said that was a great idea.

For our reflection meeting, Mary began, "I think it went well. I mean, all the kids were working just fine. I thought about what happened last time and I decided to have fewer children doing this project. I also only invited one of those boys and sat him next to two kids who are really hard workers. I got to walk around the table more, and when I worked with the little girl, I was able to help her and keep my eye on the rest of them. I think I found something they're really interested in and that helps too."

I told her that I thought it went well too. "I especially liked how you reflected-in-action when one child wanted to make a book and you encouraged her. I also thought having some-thing tangible for them to use was a great way to let them move without really being distracted." Mary added, "Yeah, and even the boy who was having trouble at the math table last time worked straight through. Maybe that's because it's something he really enjoys doing." I answered, "And maybe it's because they had time and space to do it in. I like that you only asked questions after the children spoke, and that when children asked you something, your questions redirected them to go to a book and look up the answer, letting them know they could be in charge of their own learning."

Mary and I planned for the next observation. "I think I'd like to try a large group again. I want to lead a meeting and will probably read a book about the solar system."

On our third observation, the children were on the rug and Mary was seated in the teacher's rocking chair, reading a story about a wayward star. The children were attentive although I thought the story went on too long. Mary then asked questions about some of the vocabulary used in the book, and the children eagerly responded. She wrote these on a language chart and said, "We'll keep those words up here in case anyone wants to use them in their stories. Does anyone have any questions?" One precocious child raised his hand and said, "I always wanted to ask this question: What's inside the earth?" Mary smiled broadly and said, "I don't know. That's certainly something we could find out together. When meeting is over, let's go see if there's a book that will tell us more about that." Mary then sent the children to different tables to work on some planet-related photocopied sheets. Again, the children had to either use a book or ask a buddy if they didn't know the answers. And, since the whole class did this at the same time, Mary had arranged for the cooperating teacher and the assistant teacher to sit at tables and help children.

"So how do you think it went?" I asked as usual. "I think the meeting was fine. I wanted to use vocabulary from the book, but I thought the book itself wasn't so interesting. I think the children liked it though. Maybe the meeting went on a little too long. I saw some kids starting to get antsy. And even though that question at the end was great, I didn't want to start another whole lesson then. I think when it's my classroom, I won't have all the children do the same thing at the same time. I'd let them choose to do a worksheet as part of the whole work time. It got so hectic even though I worked it out for the other teachers to help. People were finished at different times and I didn't have anything else for them to do. I sent them to read a book, but that seemed not to last as long as I needed it to. I guess you saw me looking a little desperate. Thanks for sitting with those two girls. That really helped since they usually need more time."

I said, "No problem. Sometimes it's hard not to jump in . . . but in this case you were running all over the room and the other teachers were also busy. You know, you've hit the nail right on the head with your reflection. I think you have really gotten good at reflecting on your work. I would have said the same thing to you about this observation. Teaching takes practice like anything else you'd want to become good at. Again, the kids took it in stride, especially since Justine's style is to allow for noise and movement. She's less organized and more spontaneous, but then again she has years of experience. I think you're going to do just fine, as long as you keep using reflection as a tool to look at your practice. I think you already have that skill."

- Have you ever been observed on the job? Was it for an evaluation or supervision? Who observed? What happened after the observation?
- Did you agree with the other person's comments? Why or why not?
- Were you satisfied by the format used? Why or why not?
- Think about the ways you have responded to children's work or questions that are examples of reflecting-in-action.
- Think about changes you have made in a lesson or planned experience that show reflection-on-action.
- Have you had opportunities to reflect-for-action? What did you do? Were you successful?

On the Job: Directors or Principals, Colleagues, and Consultants

Directors or Principals

A productive mentored relationship with the director or principal where you work has the potential to be one of the most rewarding professional connections you could develop. While successful learning about theories of education and how to put them into practice will start with your college mentor, your ongoing growth and job satisfaction after you graduate will depend on the quality of your relationship with your boss.

I am not talking here about friendship. That might be an outgrowth of your professional relationship and would be a bonus if it should develop. But often directors and principals are not meant to be your friend. They are meant to lead your institution. If they are good leaders, they will support your desire to learn new things or to try new approaches in your classroom. They will also inevitably make decisions with which you do not agree. And that is the hardest place to be if your boss is your friend.

A good site leader, be it a principal, director, vice principal, educational director, or area specialist, will offer you many of the same supports that a field supervisor or professor will. On-the-job mentoring will be different in that it is meant as "on-the-job training." This can sometimes take on the added weight of evaluation. Evaluation can take two forms: summative evaluation and formative evaluation (Stake 1967). Summative evaluation has more to do with the functioning of the organization. It is used to evaluate someone's performance and worth, and to compare and sort out by reward or punishment (Bey and Holmes 1990). Formative evaluation, on the other hand, should assist you in your progress toward becoming an excellent teacher. Much like supervision, the goal of formative evaluation is for you and your mentor to identify your strengths and weaknesses, relying on the former and working on strategies to address the latter.

Hopefully, your director will have been trained in some aspects of supervision or mentoring. You would also hope that your director or principal has expert knowledge in early childhood pedagogies and has created an atmosphere of respect, trust, and security for all who work in this setting. Hopefully, too, she or he has fostered a culture of professional expectations and behaviors. These should be clearly articulated and referred to often during staff meetings, team meetings, and meetings between teachers and parents.

"Family-style" Meal Times

I remember when I was directing a day care center and the furniture in each of the classrooms was set up the same way. All of the tables were pushed together in the center, creating one large tabletop. The activity areas of the classroom were against the walls, with little or no definition between them. Chairs were positioned so they knocked down block buildings. During work time, children cooked, painted, and used manipulatives at these tables, all at the same time.

When I asked about this setup, one teacher told me that the regional consultant said that the children and staff must eat their lunch together "family style." The consultant gave a directive and the staff obeyed. To this group of teachers, "family style" meant that everyone was at the same table, and the only way to accomplish this was to push all the tables together.

No one had ever thought to go back to these teachers and revisit what this directive meant to them. No one questioned the consultant. No one assumed that supervision was anything other than authoritarian. So these teachers and children lived in these classrooms, struggling daily with awkward furniture arrangements, being frustrated by not having enough room in each of the areas, and having to contend with children walking around all of the tables to get from one place in the classroom to another.

When we met as a faculty, we raised questions about the ways the rooms functioned and we shared our understanding of what "family-style" meals meant at home and in a classroom setting. We agreed that at home people usually eat at the same table, but at school this didn't seem to work when you consider the layout of the classroom. We agreed that the most important aspect of "family-style" meals was that the teachers sat with the children as they ate, presented food in containers so that the children could serve themselves and share, and everyone, children and teachers alike, could talk to one another during the meal. We drew maps of the classrooms as they were and then drew maps of the classrooms as the teachers would like them to be. Then we moved tables and furniture. And the fact that I would take responsibility for the changes in room arrangements when the consultant came freed the teachers from arbitrary restrictions and fear of reprisals.

As the director, my role was to offer the staff opportunities to discuss their work, their understanding of that work, and what they wanted to see happen as their work continued. My supervisory role was to help organize and bring people together to discuss issues that affected their work. Classroom furniture arrangement was a very concrete way to begin.

Soon after this change took place, I began to meet with the individual teaching teams on a regular schedule. Sometimes we talked about children. Sometimes we talked about curriculum. Sometimes we talked about motherhood. But what we did at those meetings was develop a sense of purpose, not just for each classroom but for each teacher as a professional. We began to scaffold new learning about early childhood education onto what we already knew and to see how those ideas fit into the child care setting in which we worked. And from there, we began clinical supervision.

Being mentored by your director can have the added benefits that your daily interactions provide. Usually you will not need to wait so long for feedback. The director should be familiar with the children in your class, and can be on hand to support you, for example, meeting with parents, when you need it. She will have firsthand experience with aspects of the program that run smoothly, and with challenges you may face.

Another important role that your director/mentor may play is as a role model. By being an integral part of the center's team, she should be part of your classroom as well. For example, when I was a nursery school teacher, the staff asked if we could hire someone to come in and lead music sessions with the children. Since the director knew we didn't have the budget for this, she, being a musician, took on the role. She came into each classroom every other week and led the children in music and movement, using rhythm instruments and children's books as complements to singing.

Not only did I learn many children's songs and ideas for creative movement exercises, I learned about discipline and full group management. I learned about reading stories and about their dramatization. I learned by observing her and, most importantly, by talking about my impressions afterward. Again, in an atmosphere of respect and openness, we were able to learn together.

In some settings, your director or principal may be expected to keep written records of your performance. This evaluative approach sometimes takes precedence over a supervisory approach. Perhaps there aren't enough administrators to work intensively with the teaching staff. Perhaps this isn't a priority in your setting. If the only times you see your director or principal are for evaluation, find someone else to be your mentor. If you are lucky, you will have other, more experienced teachers who are willing to take on this role for you.

Colleagues

When teachers mentor teachers, this is called peer mentoring or peer supervision. Teachers who are new to the field, assistant teachers who have moved into lead teacher positions, and teachers who have taught older children and are now working in early childhood classrooms would all benefit from a mentoring relationship. Peer mentoring may be an excellent choice to get "on-the-job training" without the pressures often associated with having a boss supervise you. Teachers who are ready to mentor are usually excited by the prospect of sharing their expertise and consider this an opportunity to further their own professional development.

As with any mentor, you want to find someone who is not new to the field. Remembering Katz's (1972) and Vander Ven's (1988) identified stages of early childhood teacher development might help you identify a colleague who can take on a mentoring relationship. Obviously teachers who are in the latter stages would make better mentors. Teachers who are able to consolidate beliefs about teaching, classroom management, and family/teacher partnerships, those who are ready for renewal and want to integrate outside interests into their classroom practice, or the mature teacher who has even more experience and is ready to teach other adults make great classroom mentors. She should also be someone who can model the kind of teacher you wish to become and should encompass the qualities that *you* believe make a good teacher.

Whether you seek out a peer mentor or one is assigned to you, remember that this is a professional relationship. As you would in any mentored relationship, be clear about your goals and how you would like to reach them. Use many of the same techniques you used in your student teaching placement, developing a cycle where you can plan, collaborate, follow through, and reflect together.

Set a schedule for meeting times. Since both of you will be teaching your own classes, you will need to schedule times to observe your mentor, for her to observe you, and for you both to discuss what you each have learned.

Be clear about your roles and the roles that your administration might play in this process. You may want to ensure confidentiality about your discussions and reflections.

Box 4-5

Dispositions of effective master teachers

- How much they enjoy working with young children is readily apparent in their ongoing curiosity about children's development and ideas.
- They value children's play as a cornerstone of learning.
- They expect change and want to be challenged.
- They are willing to take risks and make mistakes.
- They practice self-reflection and are open to others' suggestions.
- They actively seek collaboration, accepting and giving peer support. (Carter and Curtis 1994)

Say this upfront. Remember, one of the cornerstones of a good mentoring relationship is the ability to speak freely, without judgment or fear of reprisal. At the same time, do not assume that you can be totally informal until you are given cues that, for example, talking about your personal life outside of school is acceptable.

And, finally, show appreciation. Although your peer mentor may also be benefiting professionally from this experience, she is most likely not receiving any other compensation for her efforts. Again, I do not mean that you should ignore boundaries or be overly solicitous. At the very least, say thank-you often.

Consultants

What is an early childhood educational consultant? In different settings, this can take on different meanings. Educational consultants can either be hired by your director or principal or assigned to your center or school by a governing agency. The consultant's job description can range from evaluator to workshop leader to teacher trainer to program developer.

A consultant who is hired by your director or principal is usually an expert in a content-specific area or in some aspect of organizational management. Often this type of consultant will run professional development workshops but may also be enlisted to do program assessment. For example, as many child care settings are opting to become accredited by the National Association for the Education of Young Children, a consultant may be hired to mentor the center director as she works with the staff in preparation for meeting the accreditation criteria. Therefore, this kind of consultant will probably be on-site at a regularly scheduled time and may be accessible to you should you want her help.

Consultants that are employed by governing agencies, a department of education, for example, will most likely be assigned to your site by that agency. This consultant's role is often to ensure that the mandates, curriculum, and practices as outlined by the governing agency are being carried out in the classroom. Hopefully, this consultant will not only evaluate your program and individual classrooms but will be available to help you achieve those mandated curricular goals. Unfortunately, many governing agencies are understaffed in this area, and your consultant will not be available to spend the time needed for ongoing, one-on-one supervision.

It is not often that a classroom teacher is mentored by a consultant. But should you be lucky enough to develop a relationship with a good early childhood educational consultant, you should make the most of the time you will spend together. As you would for any professional meeting, be prepared before you approach the consultant. Are there specific questions you would like to ask? Write them down. Do you want feedback on specific areas of the room? Make an appointment so that she can set aside time to visit your room. Would you like to follow up on something she taught in a workshop? Let her know what you may have tried so far and perhaps she can help you with what you should do next.

If she cannot spend time with you, hopefully she can serve as a resource for you, suggesting specific books or materials or Internet sources. Perhaps too, like the relationship Ramon developed with his UPK consultant, you will learn by teaching. By educating the consultant about why you do what you do, you will reinforce your own "best practices," reflect on what you do in light of what you will explain to her, and remain secure in your understandings of early childhood education.

Social Supports: Family, Friends, and Fellow Students

Your mentor may be outside the university altogether. He or she may be someone who has supported you in other areas of your life. Your mentor might not know much about teaching but might know a lot about you. Most likely, this support person will have been in place before you began college and will be there after you finish. Perhaps this person may not be able to offer you much in the way of academic insights or ideas about how to run a classroom, but can instead give you the kinds of supports you need while you figure out the rest.

Parents or other family members are your first teachers. They are the people with whom you have had your first social interactions. They teach you your first languages, not only verbal utterances but also the ways you engage with others through eye contact, touch, pace, and turn taking. They impart their belief systems, notions of responsibility, expectations, values, and ways of dealing with hardship or success.

For some, your families offer mentorship throughout your lives, including guidance in education through the college years. They can refer to their own college experiences and offer insights into navigating the bureaucracies and red tape required for registration or financial aid. They "speak" the academic language and understand what is expected in this setting. They can offer advice on writing, or can tell you where to go to get the extra help you might need. They are aware of college life and accept what you are going through as part of the process of becoming the fully realized person you want to be.

For others, your families may not have had the opportunities afforded by higher education. Although they may be delighted and extremely proud of your choice and hard work in college, they may not be able to help you navigate through a university system. While they may support you, they cannot guide you in choosing classes or writing college level papers. And, as supportive as they might be, they may even question the efficacy of your decision to pursue a college degree.

Family and other social supports differ from each other and are often filled by different people in your life. For example, "(a) *Instrumental support* includes practical kinds of help or tangible aid, such as financial assistance, that is provided by family or friends; (b) *informational supports* consists of information and advice that help an individual cope with personal problems; and (c) *appraisal support* includes praise and validation that bolster an individual's self-evaluation" (House 1981, cited in Bauman, Wang, DeLeon, Kafentzis, Zavala-Lopez, and Lindsey 2004, 13, italics in original).

While your friends or family might not fully understand your academic goals, they are probably willing to help in some way. Family members are most often the ones to give you instrumental support (Bauman et al. 2004). They can offer immediate help with emergencies or child care, or long-term assistance, such as emotional or monetary support. For example, as someone who teaches courses in the evenings, I've heard countless students say during class that "the kids are with my mother."

While emergency supports will hopefully be called upon rarely, be sure that you have arranged for those supports to be in place should you need them. Long-term supports will need to be negotiated over time. Those making a long-term commitment to your development most likely will be people closest to you. Again, they probably knew you before you began college and will stay connected to you long after you graduate.

For informational support, having a secondary mentor may be helpful within the university, your student-teaching placement, or your work environment. This secondary mentor might be an academic advisor, helping you organize your undergraduate studies. She might advise you on your relationship with professors in the program and direct you to a faculty member who can take you on as a mentee.

Other secondary supports may be found. For example, during your student-teaching placement you will probably be placed in a cooperating school with other student teachers. This is a conscious decision on the part of your program director. Being in someone else's classroom can be intimidating enough; being "alone" in a school can be overwhelming. Get to know the other student teachers. Most likely, you will have an idea who they are, having seen them in other early childhood education courses during your studies. Try to meet with them for lunch or during a break. Discuss what your experiences have been so far. Ask them to talk about their cooperating teacher. These kinds of informal conversations are actually what we in the field call "teacher talk." It is the way we share information about all kinds of job-related events. It often takes place in the teachers' lunchroom, where everyone can relax and share what they're really feeling. Knowing what others' experiences are can help you gage your own. Just be sure to sort real issues from vindictive or baseless complaints—you wouldn't want to get caught up in someone else's unproductive behaviors.

Remember, as in your mentored relationship, both you and the people in your support network will need to benefit from the relationship. Don't ignore what *they* may need that you can provide. People are more willing to give when they also receive.

Being Assertive: Getting What You Need Using DERM

It is important that you are clear about your goals and what you may need from your mentor in order to achieve these goals. This is not to say that you will always know what it is you need—actually you are being mentored so that another, more experienced person can guide you to define your needs and help you develop strategies to meet them.

One of the most useful techniques I have learned is how to be assertive. First, I had to learn the difference between being assertive and being aggressive. I always thought that in order to get what you needed or wanted, you should go after it aggressively. But what I learned was that when you assume an aggressive stance, others tend to take a defensive position. Therefore, you meet up with resistance, since no one wants to feel like he or she has to give something up, especially to a bully. So, being aggressive was being counterproductive—or at least creating an adversarial atmosphere when one wasn't necessarily needed.

Being assertive is a way to present and ask for what you need without putting the other person on the defensive. This is an important skill that can help create good communication with your mentor, or anyone else for that matter. An effective way of doing this is to use "I" statements, which make it clear that the desire or need is yours alone, and that if the other person wants to join with you, the overall outcome could be beneficial to all. Learning a technique called DERM will come in handy, especially in situations where you may not feel so confident about speaking up or when what you need to say may be difficult for the other person to hear.

DERM

The acronym DERM stands for:

DESCRIBE: from an *objective* stance, **describe** what has occurred (this is based on the facts of a given incident). For example, "Yesterday at our meeting, I raised several concerns that didn't get addressed. There seemed to be so many other people around that it was difficult to talk."

EXPRESS: express how you felt in this situation using "I" statements only. For example, "*I* was disappointed that we didn't get to talk about these issues." Say only how you felt, not what you *think* the other person felt or what you *imagine* his or her motives to be. You don't *know* what the person thought, and it really doesn't matter right now. This is about what *you* need.

REQUEST: ask for what you need. For example, "Perhaps we can meet in your office instead of in the cafeteria." Again, stay fact-based and be direct. You are making a request here, not blaming and certainly not demanding. What you must understand, though, is that the other person *has the right* to refuse your request. He or she has needs too.

MOTIVATE: This may be the trickiest part, but if done right, you have **presented a win-win situation** and there's less resistance to your idea. For example, "In looking at the amount of work I have to review, I would like to be able to schedule at least an hour of uninterrupted time with you to discuss it before I can go on with my project." Here you show that you are serious about doing the work, that you have come prepared, that you are taking responsibility for the quality of the work, that you value the mentor's time as well as your own, and that you are flexible and understand that you are negotiating someone else's time, but that you are standing your ground and not forgoing *what you need.*

Finally, make sure you come to closure and that you both have the same understanding of what it is you have agreed to. Repeat what you hear, and write it down.

Nina

Nina, a twenty-four-year-old early childhood education graduate had recently been hired as the lead teacher for a pre-K class in a small nursery school. As a young head teacher, she was paired with an assistant who had been working in this school for three years but had done no academic work in early childhood education. Nina found herself doing all of the planning, the one-on-one interactions with children, and all of the written observations. She was exasperated by having to ask the assistant for help, especially when she had to give her attention to one individual child while the other children waited and often grew impatient.

Nina found herself being curt and practically giving orders to the assistant. She worried that this tone would spill over into her interactions with the children. Often, at the end of the day, Nina went home exhausted, frustrated, and feeling like she did not want to go back to work. She couldn't understand why the assistant just didn't do what was needed. By the fourth week of school, Nina expected the assistant to know what she wanted done in the classroom and was taken aback when, after children made their work choices, the assistant told her, "That's not how we do it in this school." And, since Nina had a college degree in early childhood education, she expected the assistant's unconditional respect.

- What questions might you ask Nina to uncover more about this situation?
- What questions might you ask the assistant teacher?
- What "rights" does Nina have as the lead teacher? How would these influence her expectations?
- What "rights" does the assistant have? How would these influence her expectations?
- What are some of Nina's behaviors that are hindering the relationship? How could Nina get what she needs?
- Role play this scenario using DERM.

DERM does not come easily. It has to be practiced, and it can and should be rehearsed. It might not work. It may sound corny. But, once you understand why it's a good communication tool, and you become comfortable with it, you can devise your own shorthand for how to use it. And hopefully you will, even if only to help yourself get organized and centered and clear about what you want before you ask for it.

Identifying Challenges in Mentored Relationships

A discussion of common challenges posed: how to identify them, and ways to try to resolve them

❖ Identifying Your Own Learning Styles
❖ Motivation
❖ Making the Match or Finding Your Complement
❖ Working with Mentors Who Are Different from You: Ethnicity, Gender, and Age

Identifying Your Own Learning Styles

Understanding how cultures and prior experiences influence approaches to learning will help you to recognize characteristics of your own learning styles. The challenge here is to remember that the dominant culture in college settings will dictate the preferred learning styles, and as a result, assignments, activities, and lectures will reflect these preferences.

There are numerous theories and attitudes regarding learning styles, including cognitive, sociocultural, gender-based, and stage theories, to name a few. The term "learning styles" suggests the many ways you bring together your thinking about and your emotional reactions to subjects. This includes the particular ways you think when you are in the act of learning, the ways you think about learning, and the ways you feel most comfortable learning (Vermunt and Vermetten 2004).

Another way to think about learning styles is to use Lev Vygotsky's (1978) sociocultural theory of learning, in which he maintained that all learning is socially mediated. Vygotsky was interested in the relationship between the development of language and thought (1986). He believed that learning was nonlinear, meaning that you do not learn something once and move on. For Vygotsky, as well as other constructivist theorists, since you are an active participant in your own learning, you revisit experiences building on what you already know, intensifying different ways of understanding a concept or experience. For Vygotsky, learning does not occur in set stages. Importantly, he believed that in order "to learn concepts, the learner must experience them and *socially negotiate* their meaning in the authentic context of a complex learning environment" (Jaramillo 1996, 135, italics added). What you take from an experience, what you learn from it, is dependent upon cultural and social ways of knowing.

As part of his cultural-historical approach, Vygotsky proposed that there are three facets to learning: advanced cognitive functions, culturally significant influences on development, and the management of one's own actions and performance. From cognitive and cultural standpoints, thinking, learning, and ways of viewing the world are shaped by social experience, especially learning as part of a family and particular culture. From the behavioral standpoint, you will tend to seek out situations that are compatible with the ways you learn best.

Because the definition of a culture includes what is shared by people who make up that culture, learning "how to learn" includes the ways you speak (and this is certainly different in different contexts) and listen, record and transmit information, and what you consider beautiful or just. This is not to say that everyone from a particular culture will learn and think in exactly the same ways. But since culture is learned and shared, there are common patterns of what is deemed important to know and how it is learned. For Vygotsky (1986) these ways of making meaning, interacting, and behaving in the world are interrelated and inseparable.

Institutions where good mentoring takes place help learners become mindful of their particular strengths, or intelligences. Along these lines, it would also be helpful to look at Howard Gardner's theory of multiple intelligences (1983), whose principal applications focus on K–12th graders. Gardner, a scholar at Harvard University, suggests that all learners have specific strengths through which they find it easier to learn, solve problems, and create. For example, you may be a tactile learner, needing to be able to touch or manipulate objects to truly understand a concept. You may have interpersonal skills and your strengths lie in your ability to work with other people. Or you may have an affinity for understanding objects in relation to one another, therefore portraying a spatial intelligence. Gardner lists more intelligences, but for now, what is most important is his belief that teachers should use these intelligences as assets to facilitate and deepen a student's learning. Identifying your own intelligences will position you to use your strengths in familiar frameworks and to develop strategies when you must learn outside your comfort zone. Remember that although there may be times when you will need content-specific tutoring for subject areas outside of your education courses, the relationships between attitudes and behavior are associated with personal beliefs and not cognitive ability. The skills you have developed in order to identify, initiate, and engage in a mentoring relationship should serve you well as you put these to work in finding a subject-specific tutor. Remember also that students who resist giving in to setbacks or obstructions often attribute their success to previous experiences and their perseverance beyond school settings (Eppler and Harju 1997).

Interestingly, Sandra Kerka (2000) points to the growing literature and applications of multiple intelligences geared toward adults. Shearer (1998) created an adult version of a multiple intelligences assessment, adding three scales that describe intellectual styles such as leadership, innovation, and general logic. Importantly, Kerka notes that most of the work done on adult multiple intelligences focuses on three areas: (1) adult literacy learners and adults with learning disabilities who may have experienced early schooling failure because they were labeled by earlier, more limited conceptions of intelligence; (2) workplace applications of multiple intelligences to increase creativity and productivity by enabling workers to use their strengths; and (3) connecting multiple

---

Box 5-1

Think about how each of the following influence how you learn:

- The environment's impact on your learning—including temperature, sound, lighting and design
- Your emotional state or temperament—including persistence, motivation, organization, and responsibility
- The impact of sociocultural ways of looking at the world—this category includes socially influenced patterns in which learning occurs, such as learning alone or in groups, or having an orientation to authority or to peers
- The ways in which your physiological needs impact learning—having hunger or physical comfort needs met, time of day, learning through touch and manipulation, auditory or visual learning, or needing to be in motion
- A psychological learning style—referring to the ways you sort out information and ideas (using a divergent or global approach compared to a convergent or analytical approach), your ability to learn in a cooperative and noncompetitive setting, and/or having internal or external control (being self-motivated or responding better to others' expectations or deadlines)

---

intelligences and diverse learning styles using technologies such as the computers or the Internet.

Since one of the major goals is to help you work toward increasing academic achievement and developing a greater commitment to learning, a good mentor should be aware of your learning styles. According to Griggs and Dunn (1995), teachers and counselors should attend to students' preferences. While the authors of this study focused on Latino/a learning styles, they listed five general categories of styles that mentors should understand and acknowledge. These include the environment, your emotional state, the impacts of social and cultural influences, your physiological needs, and your psychological styles.

In helping you to recognize your learning styles so that you can actively influence learning environments, and how you and your mentor approach your work together, consider the following "Inventory of Learning Styles" developed by Vermunt and Vermetten (2004, 365). For me it isn't so important to memorize the headings, but it is important to understand that we all use different strategies to learn different things.

Try to identify which of these strategies, conceptions, and orientations best fit your current ways of learning and if there are any styles you might like to develop.

Processing Strategies

- *Deep processing* occurs when you *relate* components of information to each other, and *structure* these into a whole. *Critical processing* is another strategy in which you draw your own conclusions about the subject and are

TABLE 5-1

Inventory of Learning Styles

	Deep	*Stepwise*	*Concrete*		
How you **process** information	–connect pieces of information to make a whole –critically assess conclusions	–memorization and rehearsal –analyze details	–apply information to your experience		
	Self-regulation	*External regulation*	*Lack of regulation*		
How you **regulate** your learning	–plan activities –check progress –test outcomes –adjust and reflect –consult others	–others decide what you will learn and how you will learn it	–little or no control over your learning		
	Constructivism	*Intake knowledge*	*Using knowledge*	*Stimulating*	*Cooperative*
Concepts about learning/ knowledge	–learn by doing: activities, experience, insights	–learn by taking in others' knowledge –memorize and reproduce knowledge provided by others	–learner and teacher together apply knowledge to real situations	–teacher and text incite and inspire active learning	–tasks and understandings are shared –all learners succeed
	Personal interests	*Goal orientation*	*Ambivalence*		
Why you learn	–subject matter interests you –learning for self-improvement	–often related to job or certification requirements	–question your goals –second-guess your abilities –concern about type and quality of education: style and content		

(Adapted from Vermunt and Vermetten 2004)

critical of the conclusions presented by others, including texts and teachers' opinions.

- *Stepwise processing* occurs when you learn facts, definitions, and lists by heart by *memorizing and rehearsing* them. *Analyzing* occurs when you study the separate elements of subject matter one by one and in detail.
- *Concrete processing* occurs when you *apply* subject matter to your own experiences and *practice* what is learned.

Regulation Strategies

- *Self-regulation* occurs when you *plan* learning activities, *check* your progress, *test* the outcomes, *adjust*, and *reflect.* You also self-regulate when you *consult* supporting literature and outside sources.
- *External regulation* occurs when you let outside sources regulate your learning processes. For example, learning is confined to teachers' objectives, directions, questions, or assignments.
- *Lack of regulation* occurs when you find it difficult or nearly impossible to actively participate in or control your own learning processes.

Concepts of Learning

- *Construction of knowledge* occurs when learning activities are seen as *tasks of the learner.* Learning occurs when you construct your own knowledge through *experience and insights.*
- *Intake of knowledge* occurs when learning is seen as *taking in knowledge provided by others* and is *memorized and reproduced.* Learning activities are seen as the *tasks of teachers,* not learners.
- *Use of knowledge* is seen as both the *tasks of learners and teachers together.* Learning is viewed as acquiring knowledge that can be made concrete by its application.
- *Stimulating education* occurs when teachers and texts continuously stimulate and challenge the learner although the learning activities are seen as the students' tasks.
- *Cooperative learning* occurs when learning is seen as a cooperative effort, *tasks and understandings are shared, so everyone succeeds.*

Learning Orientations

- *Personally interested* is studying because you are *interested* in the subject and wish to develop yourself as a learned person.
- *Certificate or vocation orientation* is studying because you wish to pass examinations, get credits or a degree. These are often job related.
- *Ambivalence* occurs when you are uncertain about your studies, your capabilities, the type of education you are receiving, and so on.

Chantel

Chantel had heard that this was going to be an easy transition. The bachelor's program was only a few blocks from the community college, so she'd be familiar with the neighborhood, and all their courses were in the evening and on Saturday. And they had an early childhood program. She thought, "If I could register for five courses a semester, I'll be out in no time."

Chantel enrolled in the introductory early childhood course and in the language and literacy course, both of which I was teaching at the time. Her comments and questions in class added much to the discussions. She had solid background knowledge of child development and a lot of experience in classrooms with three- and four-year-olds. But, when Chantel handed in her first paper, it was obvious that she needed help with her writing. I asked to meet with her.

When she came to see me, she said, "I want to do this program as fast as I can. I need to get certified and be a head teacher for two reasons; one, for more money, and two, my director needs me to get certified so the center can get licensed. I figure, I've already done the community college program, gotten my A.A. I just want to get it all done."

I asked her to talk a little more about her experience in the community college. She was effusive about the program. She said she had learned so much about young children and that she was permitted to use her job site for fieldwork, hinting that she would like to use it for her student teaching as well. She spoke about how she understood the importance of play for young children. She mentioned that this had influenced how she interacted with her six-year-old niece. "But," she said, "I need some advice about what to do with her. Her teachers keep telling her mother that she's behind in her work, even though she seems to enjoy going to school and loves to read."

I asked Chantel to tell me about her niece's work and more about what the teachers had said. She described her niece as a lively child, curious, and funny. She just couldn't understand what the teachers were complaining about. According to Chantel, the school spoke to the child's mother and initiated a discussion about having her daughter evaluated. Chantel hesitated and said, "But I'm not sure her mother's going to do anything yet. She thinks my niece is fine." I suggested that she, being a teacher herself, try to do a more formal observation of her niece, to get a copy of her written work or one of her drawings, and to approach her questions from a professional viewpoint. She said she'd never thought of doing this but would try it.

Then I turned to her and asked about her own writing. Had anyone ever spoken with her about it before? How was the feedback from the instructors at the community college?

Chantel seemed startled. She sat up straight and said, "No one ever said anything about my writing. Well, maybe a couple of years back. But I thought I had worked on that."

"I know you want to graduate on the fast track. But I also know how smart you are. The quality of your work is OK, but there seems to be a pattern in the kinds of writing errors you're making. Let's continue to meet during the semester and work on this. One of the first things I'd like you to try is to read your papers out loud to yourself. Or if you can, have someone read them aloud to you without making any changes in the way you wrote them. Maybe if you hear what you wrote, it'll help you 'tune in,' so to speak, to your mistakes."

Chantel agreed to try this and we made an appointment to meet in two weeks.

At the next meeting, Chantel started by asking me, "Is my writing OK yet?" I said that her ideas were clear but that there were still the same types of errors. I asked if she'd tried reading aloud and she said, no she hadn't, that it was "kind of corny." I told her that I knew what she meant, since I had to do this same thing when I took a speech class and was told to practice in front of a mirror, but that I made sure the door was closed and no one could see me doing this.

I asked about her other courses and how she was doing in them. She said she was managing but that some of the professors "go so fast—it's like they expect you to know it before you learn it." I asked what she meant. She explained, "I can't keep up with taking notes, I just can't write that fast." I asked her to think about how she learns about individual children in her class. She said she watches them and sometimes she takes notes or photos of what they're doing. She said she has created a kind of shorthand for certain words that are usually in her observations. I wondered if she had tried using this technique in her courses, since there are many words that can be left out in note taking and many that are easy to abbreviate. She said she'd tried this but it was still too fast. I asked if she would consider asking her professors if she could tape-record the class and go over the tape later. Surprisingly, she came to class the next week and asked me if she could tape the session.

Before Chantel left, I turned the discussion back to her desire to "get out as soon as possible." We talked about learning and teaching, and then about what it meant to go through the program as quickly as possible instead of taking one's time to learn deeply.

At one point during our second meeting, I told Chantel that she should withdraw from the language and literacy course, which should not have been taken at the same time as the introductory course. I felt that she needed to work on her writing, and as I later found out, on her other courses. I told her that I thought she should slow down, stop rushing to be finished, that she "should get her money's worth" out of her undergraduate experience.

Still, Chantel left my office upset with me, to say the least, for not letting her continue on her own idea of the "fast track" and asking her to slow down and learn differently.

- Think about a subject or activity that you learned without much effort. What was easy about it? How did you go about learning it?
- Now, think about an area that was difficult for you to learn. What aspects of it were challenging for you? How did you go about learning it?
- Try to write your full name with the hand you don't normally use for writing. Now do it again but look only at your own hand in a mirror while you write. How did these different ways of writing make you feel?
- How can being mentored help you understand the different ways children and adults learn?

About two months into the semester, I asked Chantel if she was doing her field observations for the introductory course in her own center. She said yes, in her own classroom. I told her that I was concerned about some of the things I was reading in her observations, that I didn't think she was getting to see anything different from what she'd always done. "I think you need to see other people teach. You said your director was waiting for you to get certified so the center would be licensed? Are there any other certified teachers? Is there any other teacher you could observe?"

"Don't start me talking about my job. There's so much going on there that I think is not OK. But I've been there for two years and I can't afford to leave. That's why I want to keep going so fast, so I can get certified and move on." I asked her to think about some way to observe another teacher and that I would also like her to add another section to her field reports: a critique of what she saw, and how she would do it differently.

Meanwhile Chantel took her core courses. She formally applied and was accepted into the early childhood program. One year later, she returned to the language and literacy class. As the semester went along, she and I began to meet more often. We'd talk about her job, her schoolwork, her niece. One day Chantel said, "You know I was really mad at you. I wanted to get out of here so fast, I couldn't believe it. But you know something. I'm glad you and the academic advisor didn't let me keep going without checking things out. It's changed my way of looking at my classes. And I'm not taking so many classes each semester anymore. I mean, sure I've got to keep a full-time credit load for financial aid, but I'm not trying to kill myself anymore."

She added, "And my niece is getting tested. I'm thinking, 'Hey why shouldn't she get help? If that's what she needs.' I'm talking to her mother about it all the time. I try to help her see why it's OK and why it'll be good for her to get that extra help . . . I did the observations so I had some really great examples of where she needs the most help. But you know, *my* writing is still an issue. A few professors have talked to me about it. And now I can see what they mean. I tried what you told me about reading it out loud to myself. I could see more mistakes, but I guess not all of them!"

I asked her if she was ever evaluated in school. She said, "No. Never."

I spoke with her about the Center for Students with Disabilities, wondering if this might be the next step. "I'm not sure they have evaluation services there. They should. But maybe they can refer you to a diagnostic center that works with adults." Chantel said that she had tried that, without any luck. Later in the week, I spoke to the psychologist on faculty for the students and she said she didn't know of any either. It seemed hard to find a place to work with adults.

When it was time for Chantel to do her student teaching, she came and asked that I write a letter to her director explaining her request for a leave of absence. Chantel had been saving up sick days and vacation time in order to take this leave and student teach in another setting. She clearly understood what she could get from being in another setting: she would be a student without head teacher responsibilities, she would be observed and supervised daily by an experienced cooperating teacher, and she would get to work with elementary-aged children. She looked forward to this experience.

Chantel did her student teaching in an inclusive classroom in a public school in Manhattan. She worked hard and loved being in such a professional atmosphere. Chantel's field supervisor reported that Chantel was deeply engaged with the children and had a trusting relationship with her cooperating teacher. Her supervisor was impressed with Chantel's "great rapport with the children," but, again, was concerned about her writing skills. She and Chantel reworked many drafts of Chantel's final philosophy statement for her portfolio. Meanwhile, Chantel continued to investigate agencies that could help her identify her disability and develop strategies for her writing.

At the end of the year, when Chantel was about to graduate, in a reflection meeting with her supervisor, Chantel told her, "You know I was about to drop out of the program a while back. I was frustrated that I couldn't graduate sooner since I had to do required courses before I was allowed to do the early childhood courses. I thought I was being singled out and I couldn't understand why. But, I did what they told me, and I came to see that I really needed that foundation and that I was just rushing past everything. I slowed down and I took a good look around. I realized that I was thinking about teaching young children one way, you know, letting them explore and experiment and figure things out by doing, but I was considering my own education in an old way. I wanted to get the paperwork and be done with it. But now, once that door was opened, once I saw that real learning takes time and energy and thinking about it, I could never go back. I guess that's what happened to me; a door was opened and I stuck my head in, just a bit, but I couldn't stop looking around, and I'll never go back. I think I might go to graduate school and major in early childhood special education."

- Think about a time when your perceptions were challenged and later changed. What emotions did you experience? What methods did the person who persuaded you to change use? Would you use those same methods to persuade someone else to change their perceptions? Why or why not?

It is important that you remember that educational theories about learning are "not truth statements about why we do what we do. They provide a conceptual framework for us to explain how and why we learn. They are essentially based on beliefs that direct the question that each theorist proposes" (Jaramillo 1996, 134). In other words, theories themselves are framed by the social and cultural settings in which they were written. Like child development theories, no one learning theory will fit every learner or every situation. Still, you will come to identify your own learning styles and help your mentor know what ways you learn best. In describing ways that you learn, you will be structuring your interactions. A good mentor will strive to adjust to your needs, but will not lower his or her expectations. Discussions about how you have been successful will help you both learn about what you know, what you want to know, and the best ways to approach your learning so that you can achieve your goals. A good mentor will understand where these values, goals, and styles of learning intersect and how to use them to best support your development.

Motivation

As an undergraduate learning to become a teacher, motivation can come from the desire you have to work with, teach, and help others. Recognizing that you have the potential to make a difference in the lives of children and families and that in the process of critical transformative learning you will change your own life, you will also begin to

> (see yourself) as a creator that can cause something to exist or occur. Seeing a reflection of (your)self in the world is evidence of having been in the world and having mattered. This doing of the right thing or good, is what imparts meaning to existence and provides . . . a sense of identity. (Lange 2004, 136)

Motivation is also derived from the connections you make between the personal and social aspects of your life. As Lange (2004) writes, the reason that critical transformative learning exists is "to provoke a change at the . . . root of social systems" (123) in order to transform our present situations. For example, identifying with the children you teach may motivate you to critically reflect and become active on their behalf. Motivation might also come from your need to bounce back from previous experiences where "unjust or alienating relations" (123) forced you to regulate your own behaviors or expectations in order just to survive. For example, many adults who were educated in underserved schools are highly motivated to change those schools for future generations of learners. Lange calls this kind of motivation restorative learning and says that for adult students, restorative learning is even more dependable than critical transformative learning.

In Lange's study of adult learners, she found that adults appeared to be more aware of their own "inner compass, which was submerged under the deluge of adult expectations, cultural scripts, and workplace practices" (130). She notes that they already felt comfortable with the ethics they already had, but felt they needed to submerge these ethics as they learned to fit into society's expectations of them. These students felt they did not need transformation as much as they needed affirmation.

Hopefully, in a mentoring relationship you will be able to examine your own ethics as you address particular care/education settings and individual children's needs. On a broader note, you should certainly begin thinking about the ethical questions that are posed by society's assumptions of what makes teachers want to teach, its expectations of teachers' work, and its definitions of caring for and educating young children.

Making the Match or Finding Your Complement

What are some of the ways you would describe your "ideal" professor?

What are some traits of one of your "worst" professors?

College students who were asked to describe their "ideal" professor (Strage 2008) most frequently cited that he or she be knowledgeable, caring and concerned about students, and funny or entertaining. They also believed the professor should be friendly, engaging, enthusiastic, organized, helpful, clear, fair, accessible, and challenging.

Interestingly, these responses were different for traditional-age students as compared to older students. "Traditional age students, those coming directly from high school, appear to prefer a college environment that is essentially an extension of high school. Older and more experienced students appear to be more concerned about securing adequate preparations for career and life after college" (Strage 2008, 229).

Traditional students described the ideal professor as funny, an easy grader, and enthusiastic. Their "ideal" course was engaging, fun, and offered opportunities for participation in activities. Older students described their "ideal" professor as organized and flexible, while their "ideal" course was also well organized. Similarly, students who had transferred from community college also thought the "ideal" professor should be organized and fair, and the "ideal" course should be "applicable to the real world and relevant to their career interests" (Strage 2008, 228).

Strage concludes that the degree to which students were "familiar" with college did not play a significant role in their descriptions of professors or courses. Yet, older students and those from community colleges reported feeling more comfortable with their professors and more willing to use them as resources or ask for clarification of course material. This willingness to make opportunities for personal connections added to these students' confidence in their ability to succeed.

When we enter college, at whatever age, we all carry "educational baggage" with us from our previous school experiences. More importantly, we are all products of our families, our communities and cultures, and the society in which we live. This includes mentors as well as students. Since it is impossible for anyone to shed these influences entirely, it is better to sort through that baggage to access what's in it that can work for you. For example, were you taught to examine "facts" from different perspectives? Were you encouraged to investigate subjects that interested you, even if they were not part of the main lesson? Were you given opportunities to apply what you learned to real situations? Were you supported in your attempts to critically evaluate your own learning?

If your educational experiences include these skills, then you will certainly want to identify a mentor who will encourage you to keep using them. If these are not part of your educational repertoire, you may want to find someone who can support you while you learn these skills, since these skills will most likely form the foundations of the work you will do in college and particularly in classrooms with young children. Taking advantage of these skills and developing them into an educational framework can support your sense of autonomy and self-determination, can enrich your mentoring relationship, and can become important talents in your repertoire of lifelong learning.

While the higher education mentoring literature addresses issues around both cross-gender and cross-ethnicity mentoring relationships, and many formal mentoring programs tend to pair students with a mentor from their own gender or ethnic background, there is no consensus about the usefulness of these pairings (Jacobi 1991; Kochan 2002). Other "matching" traits included gender, ethnicity and language, and prior experiences, especially in relation to which grades the mentor had taught previously. While programs that attempt to match mentoring pairs look at the characteristics listed above, there is no predictor that can address the elusive and subtle qualities of a relationship.

Claire Owen and Linda Zener Soloman conducted a study in New York City public schools (2006) that looked at whether shared similarities such as teaching style, personality, and similar values would significantly and positively affect teachers' satisfaction with a *formal* mentoring program. Although attempts were made to match teachers and mentors in tangible areas such as licensing area, grade, and subject taught, similar personality traits were coincidental. The results for each of the three different years that the data were collected point to increased satisfaction with the program and a positive influence on the mentee's part to continue teaching in the NYC public schools.

Owen and Zener Soloman suggest that if informal mentoring is a choice, you should look for mentors who match your experiences in licensing, ages, and subjects taught and who seem to be most like yourself in personality and values. In formal programs, they advise that the program coordinators match students and mentors with these traits in mind.

In a study conducted in 2005, Rowena Ortiz-Walters and Lucy Gilson found that graduate students of color felt they received more psychosocial and influential mentoring from mentors who were also of color. They also reported feeling more comfortable and more satisfied in these relationships. This is noteworthy since other reviews of the mentoring literature report that these matching traits have no impact on the "success" of the mentoring relationship. Yet the authors of this study further clarify this discrepancy by pointing out that previous studies were conducted with a sample that was predominately Caucasian, while their study focused on African American, Latina/o, and Native American graduate students. Therefore, the authors argue that while similarity may not have been important to white protégés, racial/ethnic similarity was an important surface similarity for protégés of color. Finally, the authors of this study found that protégés who perceived their mentors to be more like themselves reported feeling more satisfied, comfortable, and supported.

Still, the most important thing to establish with your mentor is *trust* (Johnson-Bailey and Cervero 2002; Kay and Jacobson 1996; Martin and Trueax 1997).

Working with Mentors Who Are Different from You: Ethnicity, Gender, and Age

Regardless of background, the mentor must be willing to work hard on your behalf. She should allow you to try out ideas and skills in a safe and supportive environment. She should strive to become someone you believe is essential to your development as a teacher of young children. She should be someone who is willing to struggle with the hard questions that are part of everyday life for people working toward educational equity and social justice. Your mentor should be able to realize and support you in the various ways you self-identify. For example, a woman of color might find gender issues more pressing and may not appreciate the mentor who sees everything from a racial perspective (Scisney-Matlock and Matlock 2001).

Regardless of "the match" it is important and necessary for you both to cultivate a shared appreciation for what each of you might mean by diversity. These frank and sometimes difficult discussions will take place over time, and will change as your relationship develops. Maybe your mentor is someone who has fostered opportunities for these discussions to take place, not just on an individual basis but within her academic community. Perhaps, then, you and she will work together to be at the vanguard of change, not only in the college setting but in your early childhood classroom and work environment as well.

Although the number of nontraditional and ethnic minority undergraduate students has grown in recent years, the numbers of minority faculty have not (Bowman, Kite, Branscombe, and Williams 2000). And, in terms of the early childhood or elementary classroom, the majority of the teaching force continues to be made up of white, middle-class women. Therefore, many students new to early childhood education will be mentored by faculty, supervisors, or classroom teachers who have not experienced the prejudices faced by minorities in mainstream American culture.

For a traditional majority ethnic student who may have sought out or been paired with an ethnic minority faculty member, there will certainly be many opportunities to question assumptions and learn what it is like to see the world from his or her point of view.

For the "new" undergraduate, the mentor will need to be aware of your struggles as a nontraditional student who often does "not fit the profile of those who preceded them . . . [and] are not as easily matched with traditional placeholders, who are usually White" and who may have a hard time accepting the "established patterns of success required by particular institutions with the goal of maintaining the status-quo . . . and do not wish to conform to established rules of the game that often are discriminatory against minorities and women" (McCormick 1997, cited in Haring and Freeman 1999, 2).

The evidence is also inconclusive regarding the importance of making the match between student teacher and cooperating teacher (Haring 1999). Most studies look at matches created to encompass educational philosophies, beliefs about children and schools, ways of teaching, and how children learn. Some studies describe what happens when there is a mismatch. Graham's 1997 work found that student teachers and cooperating teachers who had different philosophies often suffered from miscommunication while their interactions tended to be tension-filled. Bunting (1988) found that students who disagreed with their cooperating teacher's beliefs about teaching showed little change or growth. At the same time, Hollingsworth's work (1989) found that students who agreed with their cooperating teachers also tended toward little change, since these students felt comfortable in their convictions, were not challenged to question their beliefs, and did not try to examine the quality of their student-teaching experience including the complexity of some of the issues they faced in these placements (cited in Burk Rodgers and Dunn 2000). Burk Rodgers and Dunn advocate instead for "cooperation that supports autonomy (and) is grounded in mutual respect . . . [where] participants consider themselves on equal footing" (20). Even if you consider yourself on equal footing to your mentor or cooperating teacher in terms of life experience, it is important to be in an "autonomy-supportive environment" (Deci, Eghrari, Patrick, and Leone 1994, cited in Burk Rodgers and Dunn 2000) where your relationship is built on cooperation and respect. Mentors and cooperating teachers that support your autonomy and self-determination will "(a) provide meaningful rationales, (b) acknowledge (your) perspective, and (c) extend an atmosphere of choice rather than control" (Burk Rodgers and Dunn 2000, 21). This would also be true for teachers who support the autonomy and self-determination of young children.

As Juanita Johnson-Bailey, an African American woman, and Ronald M. Cervero, a Caucasian man, who have worked together in a faculty mentoring relationship have said, "There is no magical transformation that occurs as teachers and learners step across the threshold of the classroom" (1997, para. 4). They argue that within the confines of most classrooms, adult learners will continue to experience the same power relations that they have known in the real world unless they actively question those relationships and act upon their findings. This will probably hold true of your mentoring relationships as well. While it is the mentor's responsibility to frame your relationship in the context of wider social issues and not just as an individual case devoid of context, it may turn out that you will teach your mentor about these connections.

Johnson-Bailey and Cervero conclude that power dynamics cannot be disregarded in any classroom. They also challenge the traditional notions of adult education as described in the work of Knowles and other adult education theorists. These traditional approaches to adult education focus on developmental constructs and do not fully consider the impacts that culture and political climate have on adult learners inside and outside the classroom. Andrea Cropper (2000) suggests that faculty and mentors respond to this reality by "locat(ing) mentoring within a personal and community empowerment context where mentors act as a critical friend who can assist with personal development while at the same time understanding the wider social issues operating in society and replicated in organizations" (602). She also suggests that engaging peer mentors may be one way to address issues of unequal power relationships. But to her, the most important aspect of mentoring is its capacity for reflexivity—sharing biography, bringing one's true identity and character to the mentoring process, and connecting the personal and the political within the context of the work.

And, naturally, in relationships where there are perceived dissimilarities, you will need time to get to know one another. There is always the potential for your relationship to provide unique learning opportunities as you share perspectives. Relatively new relationships that may start out not working well can improve over time. The assumptions that can influence your first impressions about "surface" characteristics should be reevaluated once you get to know more about underlying similarities such as values, attitudes, and beliefs.

Differences in Race and Ethnicity

To begin, I must admit that I struggled with using the term "race" as a heading for this section. I know that race is a social construct (Gregory and Sanjek 1994; Winant 1994, cited in Johnson-Bailey 2002) that is used in our society to group together people by physical appearance. I also understand the subtle and not so subtle ways that the creation of these categories implies characteristics about intelligence, physical appearance, and beliefs although there are no scientific bases to these claims. Yet, in American society, this way of categorizing individuals is used constantly. And, because I agree so strongly with Juanita Johnson-Bailey's suggestion that adult educators cannot ignore the influences that these categorizations and, therefore, the power these relations have on us all, I felt I must include this variable in order to address ". . . ranks, authorizations, honors, suspicions, and stereotypes" (Johnson-Bailey 2002, 40) that are part of the real world in which we live.

The question of "difference" should also be addressed when thinking about social relationships. Within this framework, one must ask, "Different from whom?" In our society, different has come to mean anyone who is not part of the mainstream culture, while the multiple implications of difference impact access, expectations, and how groups are valued. Hopefully, discussions around the ways in which you may differ from your mentor will become a topic you both conscientiously address, classifying "privilege . . . as a context-dependent force rather than depicting Whiteness and maleness as possessing the permanent high ground of rights and entitlements" (Johnson-Bailey 2002, 46). Both critical reflection and reflexivity will serve you well here.

As in all mentoring relationships, individual personalities will naturally influence the ways in which you behave with each other. In cross-cultural mentoring relationships, there is the added impact of differing experiences and expectations based on majority or minority status. If you are a person of color, and your mentor is not, he or she may wish to offer you the same opportunities for success that he or she experienced. But your mentor must keep in mind that gaining access to privilege does not happen just by wishing it were so. If your mentor has access to power, he or she should find ways to "open doors" for you, knowing that "a cross-cultural mentoring relationship is an affiliation between unequals who are conducting their relationship on a hostile American stage, with a societal script contrived to undermine the success of the partnership" (Johnson-Bailey and Cervero 2002, 18).

While there is a body of work addressing the mentoring of minority students, my searches produced very few articles that examined the relationships between mentors of color and white mentees. The articles that did address cross-cultural academic relationships focused on classroom interactions where the traditional, majority culture student felt privileged and assumed the right to question the ethnic minority teacher's competence, suspected an "agenda that overtly supported racial equity" (Johnson-Bailey 2002, 44), or expected the mentor to be "careful of (the student's) feelings" (Hamilton 2002, 32). I wonder then if this void in the research is a reflection of the lack of people of color in leadership positions or as faculty. And I also wonder what benefits or concerns would surface if ethnic minority faculty were to mentor white students.

There were many recommendations for minority faculty to mentor minority students. It is assumed that minority faculty should identify with minority students and that in mentoring in a homogeneous relationship, they will feel an "intense sense of fulfillment and contribution from passing along their strategies for career advancement" (Allen and Eby 2004, 132) and offer support in ways to deal with racism, classism, sexism, and so on.

Your mentoring relationship will naturally be influenced by the ways that you and your mentor perceive your motivation, background, aptitude, and ability to fit into the culture of teaching. Making assumptions along the lines of stereotyping will keep you at a distance from one another. Not addressing those stereotypes will negatively impact your ability to trust each other. Without trust, the intensity and depth to which your work can be successfully completed will be in jeopardy. It is imperative that you and your mentor see each other as individuals with unique personalities, interests, and goals and not as representative of your respective race or ethnicity.

As participants in a mentoring relationship that replicates traditional mentoring pairs, Juanita Johnson-Bailey and Ronald Cervero's work offers insights that are helpful here (2002). Although they address a mentoring relationship between college faculty, they advise that all cross-cultural mentoring pairs "spend considerable time and emotion acknowledging the burden of racism . . ." (20). They suggest that by validating and accepting each other's "cultural communication patterns, interpersonal styles, and cultural-racial-ethnic heritages" (20) you can scaffold your trust in each other. Hopefully, you and your mentor, like Johnson-Bailey and Cervero, will examine larger societal issues around hierarchical and paternalistic patterns that could occur in cross-cultural and cross-gender mentoring relationships. Hopefully, you and your mentor will be proactive and on the lookout for these patterns. As part of your reflexive partnership, both of you must examine your own cultural identities. You must learn about each other's cultures. Along these lines, not only should you value what your mentor teaches you, but she should value what you can teach her and use it to enhance the relationship.

If you are in a cross-cultural mentoring relationship or student-teaching experience, the following questions may help you assess the quality of the experience.

- Do you "see yourself" in members of the teaching staff, the administration, and the university faculty (Guyton, Saxton, and Wesche 1996)?
- Are there representations of diverse cultures visible in the curriculum of the classrooms in which you student teach? In the syllabi of the courses you are taking?
- Are there opportunities to interact with people like you?
- If you are in a homogeneous setting, how are the voices and experiences of people outside that setting represented?
- How are assumptions challenged?
- What are some of the ways you can address your concerns?
- What are some of the empowering aspects of your mentoring experience regarding cross-cultural relationships that you can take with you into an early childhood classroom?

It is important for you and your mentor to give yourself credit for taking risks to rise above systems that value one race or ethnicity over others. Within the embrace of a trusting relationship with your mentor, you will take what you have learned to children and their families, and to your peers.

Gender Differences

While you may find yourself with a mentor who is the opposite gender, you may also find that male and female mentors differ in what they see as important in the mentoring process (Heinrich 1995; Mullen, Whatley, and Kealy 2000, cited in Langer 2001). Again, referring to New York's Empire State College as an excellent example of mentorship, Langer (2001) studied faculty mentors and found that males and females mentor differently. For the male faculty, helping students attain an academic degree was the most important objective of mentoring. Only 39% of the male faculty who participated in this study responded that "facilitat(ing) growth and development of students" was critical, while 59% of the female faculty responded that "foster(ing) student self-awareness" and concerns for personal development were more important in their roles as mentors. While women may value this kind of psychosocial interpersonal relationship (Allen and Eby 2004), unfortunately this kind of mentoring is seldom seen as the best approach, especially if you are looking for career help outside of an academic setting (Hansman 1998). And since women still have lower societal status than men, female mentors are assumed to have less power and influence and less powerful professional connections. Thankfully, in the world of early childhood education, this is seldom the case.

The relational model of mentoring favored by the female faculty at Empire State College can also be seen as a feminist mentoring model. Fassinger (1997, cited in Benishek, Bieschke, Park, and Slattery 2004) proposed a model of mentoring in which your mentor recognizes the power relations that exist, openly acknowledges these differences, and uses critical understandings of power as a way to empower you. Benishek et al. add a multicultural paradigm to this model. They suggest that

> multicultural feminist mentoring be an interactive process in which differences are (a) clearly identified, (b) explored when appropriate in order to determine their relevance to the relationship and each individual's professional development, and (c) ultimately result in a relational exchange that is respectful of differences. (434)

They call for power to be shared through collaboration and respect. In this model, it is your mentor's responsibility to raise multicultural issues and to encourage you to seek out other mentors when appropriate. The framework of this relationship is built on awareness that "education/science/work/life are not value-free" (Benishek et al. 2004, 436) and that you and your mentor can challenge prohibitive mainstream values and work together for social justice.

Depictions of cross-gender mentoring relationships most often assume that a male is mentoring a female, especially in the business world. This may not be the case in education, especially in early childhood teacher education where there are so few male faculty members or classroom teachers. Since the great majority of faculty, teachers, and site directors are female, you will most likely have a female mentor. For female students, the female mentor can serve as a role model regarding ways to balance family and career responsibilities. Jipson and Munro (1997) call this "wo/mentoring," making explicit the fact that there are only women in the relationship.

When female mentors consider themselves role models, their professional demeanor, competence, and assertiveness become a source of strength for other women, as well as an example to men. The female mentor and male protégé are not often found in the business world. Allen and Eby (2004) point out that this may be an uncomfortable match and that the relationship may be under scrutiny. They suggest that the female mentor may not be able to give the male mentee the level of psychosocial mentoring she may offer other women. I would challenge this idea and suggest that if you are a man in early childhood education, you may have had more opportunities to experience nurturing yet challenging environments. Perhaps, therefore, you will be more open to the different ways that women may have of cultivating relationships and of working in the world. By sharing resources and networking, for example, women often reject male models of competition, replacing them with collaboration and cooperation, a trait one could use in classrooms with young children.

Kram (1985), who looked at mentoring in the business world, suggested how the cross-gender mentoring relationship might be compromised. She cautioned that both of you can fall into stereotypical gender-based roles, that there are inherently few opportunities for the mentor to be a role model, that the chance for intimacy and sexual concerns negatively impact trust or confidentiality, and that the team is subject to public scrutiny and peer resentment. Hopefully, since the time this list was compiled, women have struggled against gender stereotypes and have redefined what their gender can achieve. And, since Kram's initial work was published, there have been many more mentoring relationships that are less traditional than in the past. Yet you may come across assumptions and expectations of cross-gender relationships that are hard to put to rest. There is the power relation of "man to the rescue" and "woman in distress" (Feist-Price 1994) that women must be careful to resist. This can also be played out at times when you may feel silenced as "voice," or who gets to speak, is assumed by men who have been schooled to be more assertive.

Sexual attraction and tensions can also impact the relationship. Again, it is usually of more concern if a male is mentoring a female, since this replicates many of the power-laden associations that are present in society. While you will need some level of intimacy in order to approach important issues, sexual harassment can become a real concern. If there is any question about the nature of your interactions, do not hesitate to discuss the incident with someone outside the relationship. Very often, women seek other women for support and guidance when they are in situations where they may need validation or examination of their impressions. Also, do not hesitate to withdraw from the relationship if you are in any way made to feel uncomfortable.

On the other hand, some male mentors may seem much more aloof since they are concerned with the possibility of any appearance of inappropriateness. This can also impact the relationship negatively since the level of work to be accomplished may take a back seat to appearance.

Cross-gender mentoring relationships for women of color can be further complicated by discriminatory reactions to their ethnic/racial background as well as their gender. Unfortunately the dearth of faculty of color, especially women faculty of color, will make it harder for women of color to find someone who can support them while being acquainted with some of their struggles. I suggest you find someone else with experience in college, or consider using more than one mentor. If you are a woman of color and find yourself being mentored by a faculty member from the majority culture, you will certainly benefit if your mentor would "speak less, listen, invite others to speak, give credit and acknowledgments, and enable others to see depriviledging in action" (Manglitz, Johnson-Bailey, and Cervero 2005, 1268). Again, this is where reflexive practices can make your mentoring relationship a success.

Differences in Age

The traditional model of mentoring calls for an older and more experienced person to lead and instruct the younger novice. Therefore, most of the literature on mentoring uses this model as the starting point to compare other mentoring relationships.

If you are a traditional undergraduate, you will be working with an older mentor. Working with an older master teacher can be exhilarating and, at the same time, overwhelming. You may wonder if you can ever be as competent as she. While the master teacher will certainly be an excellent role model, you should keep in mind that it took her many years to develop her skills and that, as a lifelong learner, she too continues to discover new ideas and practices. Still, while she may have more life and work experiences, you may be more active in current social issues or knowledgeable about ways to use technology.

A traditional understanding of this type of relationship usually calls for the younger person to respect the older one, often just because the person is older. But respect can mean many more things than esteem or reverence. While you may in fact admire your mentor for her years in the field or her knowledge about early childhood education, the true test of respect will come as you both develop a relationship based on understanding and high regard for your differences as well as celebration of what you share.

If you are one of the "new" undergraduates, who, in early childhood education, is often the older female student, it may turn out that you are older than your mentor. You may come into the mentoring relationship knowing how to run a household, having work experience, understanding how to meet others' needs (children and family), and having a fine-tuned sense of how to creatively do all of this at the same time. As an older female student, you may feel conflicted and under pressure to meet these demands, especially if they are often at odds with each other (Home 1998). Yet some women have found greater satisfaction and success in having multiple roles (Johnson and Robinson 1999) since there are more opportunities for noticeably distinct experiences (Carney-Crompton and Tan 2002).

As a consequence, your mentor may find that your needs are more professionally driven than emotionally or personally focused. As an older student, male or female, you may consider attaining the degree for career advancement more important than personal development (Langer 2001). Therefore, you will probably need more instrumental (financial, child care, household) support. Of course, emotional supports are important too. But as a "new" undergraduate, you have already relied on your own self-efficacy, motivation, and commitment to learning when you chose to return to school. And, as someone who will enter into a mentoring relationship with many years of adult life experience, you may in fact be versed in knowing how to nurture a rich and meaningful bond with another adult.

If your mentor is younger, she will most likely be in that position because of her educational achievements or her work in early childhood education. For example, when I began to work on my doctoral degree, I was an instructor in a community college job-development program in New York City. The students, mostly women, and the occasional man, were fifty-five years old and often older. They were learning to become teachers' aides or assistant teachers in early childhood settings.

At the time, I was forty years old. While I was not unfamiliar with the demands of parenthood, work, and school, often these students considered me less mature. I started the program thinking I knew what these students needed to learn. I soon discovered that they had a lot to teach me too. The age difference was actually a generational difference that brought with it diverse ways to think about children, education, and women's roles. There were many days when the group's discussions veered away from early childhood curriculum and practices while we all learned together what it meant to have these differing viewpoints. One of the most powerful examples came when two women spoke about being both grandmothers and primary caregivers of their young grandchildren. With their additional insights, I began to see early childhood education and policy in ways that included their experiences. While the women in this course respected me for my academic abilities, I respected them for their life experiences and for their determination. I was humbled by all that I yet had to learn.

The quality of a mentoring relationship depends on many variables: how you perceive your own leaning styles and the ability of the mentor to adjust to your styles; your motivation and willingness to work hard and your mentor's motivation and willingness to help you succeed; and the personalities and dispositions you both bring to the relationship. Hopefully, with the kinds of information provided here and with your efforts at being a reflective practitioner and part of a reflexive partnership, you will be able to approach your mentor prepared to create a meaningful and productive relationship.

Continuing to Reflect and Learn

❖ **Being a Lifelong, Reflective Practitioner**
❖ **Sharing What You Know: Mentoring Others**
❖ **Teaching and Working for Social Justice**

> There is no *teaching* without *learning* . . . teaching and learning take place in such a
> way that those who teach learn, on the one hand, because they recognize previously
> learned knowledge and, on the other, because by observing how the novice
> student's curiosity works to apprehend what is taught . . . they help themselves to
> uncover uncertainties, rights, and wrongs.
>
> Paulo Freire 2005

Being a Lifelong, Reflective Practitioner

As a student of your own practice, you will have countless opportunities to imagine, experiment, reflect on, and revisit experiences in early childhood settings. There will be those wonderful "ah-ha" moments as well as those troubling "oh-no" instances. There will be times when you can't imagine doing anything else but working with young children, and there will be times when you say, "What was I thinking when I chose to do this?"

As a student of the larger world of education, you will have limitless opportunities to think about how the ways you were taught have influenced the ways you are teaching. How, for example, have your experiences as a student impacted your ideas about being a teacher? Do you know more about what kind of teacher you would like *not* to become than you do about the process of becoming a teacher (Britzman, Dippo, Searle, and Pitt 1997)? Can you imagine the things that may have been left out of your own education that you want to be sure to include as you educate others? Can you remember the wonderful things that you learned, or exciting ways you learned them, that you want to share with children?

As a student entering a profession that has experienced extremes—from benign neglect to overregulation, including a long-standing misinterpretation of experiential approaches, and the low status shared by many in the caring professions—you must ask yourself to what extent you are willing to engage in daily struggles for autonomy, respect, and a worthy wage. To rephrase William Ayers (1995), are you strong enough to defend early care and education when people who learn that you teach young children say, "Oh, that's so sweet. I guess you get to just play all day?" Being a critically reflective practitioner who shares in a reflexive partnership should help you understand this seemingly simple statement from a broader professional context. In what ways will you respond to this statement so that you represent yourself as a professional while helping others understand the importance of your work?

With that said, one might wonder why anyone would want to teach, especially young children. And this is a wonderful question, one that needs to be explored deeply and repeatedly with your mentor and with your peers. Why *do* you want to teach young children? The usual knee-jerk response is, "I love children." But I think there has got to be more. Face it, you don't love *all* children *all* the time. So, in addition to learning about early childhood education, you will need to uncover the profound meaning in what it is you want to do. You will need to focus on what it is that makes being with children enjoyable and what it is about teaching that is rewarding. Love does not occur in isolation, without daring, or without critical reflection (Freire 2005). And, with this love for children, what do you hope to accomplish for them individually *and* collectively? How will your love of children drive you to assess your own teaching? How will your love of teaching move you to influence larger American society and your local community's perceptions of education as opposed to schooling?

As you begin to develop a relationship with teaching, you can think about these kinds of questions using what you will have learned about being mentored. Developing and nurturing relationships with more experienced mentors, as well as learning alongside peers, will help you deepen your "persistent power of questioning" (Britzman et al. 1997, 16). Once you learn how to pose good questions, and to be a critically reflective partner in your mentoring relationship, you will never relinquish the power that asking questions gives you. Your mentor should support you and empower you to question, even though some of these questions will not always be comfortable or answerable. And when you are in reflexive dialogues with peers, during those times when difficult questions must be asked and uncomfortable feelings must be felt, you will support each other so that learning and change can happen.

Much as the gains you will make with young children, your own growth may not be immediately visible and can come in small, although not insignificant increments. As your mentor will contextualize her supervision, responding to your level of understanding and comfort, you too will contextualize what you learn about early childhood theories and practices. And, at the same time, the skills you will get from your own reflective practices are the same kinds of skills that will help you become good at finding the details in your observations of and interactions with young children.

Participating in collaborative inquiry is another way for you to be part of a world that values teaching that is responsive to the individual being taught, critically examines the content to be learned, and considers the context in which this will happen. The emotional "team building" that comes from a cooperative and constructive approach develops transferable skills you can take from your mentored relationship into your teaching practices. As a member of a learning community, both as an undergraduate and as a classroom teacher, you should engage in dialogues that judge the usefulness of particular practices, theories, and popular ideas about education. Questioning assumptions, considering others' experiences and perspectives, opening your capacity to learn and move toward who you will yet become should all be familiar skills gleaned from being in a mentoring relationship.

Your mentoring relationship should be dynamic. Expect change to take place as you and your mentor come to know each other better, work together to define roles and expectations, learn from one another, and share experiences together. While your undergraduate mentoring relationship is designed to help you *enter* the teaching profession, it is also meant to help you develop ways to navigate *through* the profession. In the same manner, you should develop a relationship with teaching that is dynamic and open to change. Being a teacher requires that you are constantly examining the scholarship of teaching. Once you are on the job, think about ways to set up other relationships that can support your interests when your student-teaching mentoring relationship comes to a close.

Sharing What You Know: Mentoring Others

While you may enter an early childhood classroom with an abundance of energy and earnestness as a result of having had a positive mentoring relationship, I am not recommending that you assume a leadership role immediately upon entering your first classroom as a lead teacher or if you are starting a new job. If you think about Katz's (1972) and Vander Ven's (1988) stages of early childhood teacher development, you will quickly see why you should not take on too much. You should also assess whether being a mentor is right for you. But, on the other hand, if working with a mentor sharpens your desire to nurture leadership characteristics, you can look forward to a teaching career as both a leader of children and a leader of your peers.

You may also want to consider your experiences as a student teacher before you decide if you are ready to take on a leadership role. Gonzalez Rodriguez and Sjostrom (1998) looked at the characteristics of traditional-age and older student teachers. The nontraditional students were over twenty-five years old, and although there were no students of color in this group and only one male, many were the first in their families to go to college.

In this study, the traditional-age student teachers naturally came to the field with few teaching experiences. They approached student teaching expecting it to yield immediate results and believed that to become teachers they needed to learn discrete skills. They thought more about completing a task than reflecting on it, often lacking confidence about their capabilities and goals. In keeping with a performance orientation, they saw their mistakes as deficits. Although they worked cooperatively with the classroom teacher, they perceived themselves as subordinates and did not attempt any peer-like interactions with their cooperating teachers.

On the other hand, the older students entered their student-teaching experience with a high degree of self-confidence. They took initiative and assumed the tasks of teaching from the beginning, developing shared professional connections with their cooperating teachers. They exhibited typical adult learning characteristics; they were career-focused and analytical about their experiences. They thought that learning to become a teacher was a developmental process, and they were willing to take risks and spend the time necessary to practice and learn from their mistakes. They were able to contextualize their own behaviors in relation to the culture of the school and community.

One interesting way that you might begin to think about mentoring others is to consider the responses given by high school students in a program geared toward supporting minority teens to become teachers (Yopp, Yopp, and Taylor 1992, cited in Quiocho and Rios 2000). These young adults said that there were two important and forceful elements that made a positive impact on their decision to go into teaching: having motivational presentations, especially those presented by minority speakers, and having a chance to work in classrooms in a tutoring relationship. Being a role model and a mentor in this case might involve volunteering your time to talk about your profession and your experiences as an undergraduate student and of having been mentored.

Another characteristic of the leadership potential of "new" undergraduate students in early childhood education is the fact that many teach within the community in which they live. In a review of the research on minority ethnic group teachers, Quiocho and Rios (2000) found that many of these teachers are working with children whose backgrounds are similar to their own. Educators also believe that these teachers will bring compassion and connection to their classrooms as common social and cultural experiences are shared with the children and families in these communities (Irvine 1989, cited in Quiocho and Rios 2000).

At the same time that these teachers act as role models for minority children, they bring other important and complex social, cultural, linguistic, and intellectual attitudes to all classrooms, including positive images of people of color in active leadership roles and the potential for all children to learn from people of different backgrounds. Their leadership in classrooms and in schools will certainly encourage deeper understandings of multiculturalism. And although all teachers' attitudes toward ethnicity, gender, multilingual learners, and people with varied abilities will influence children's views of their world, minority teachers often incorporate a sense of social responsibility, consciously helping children see themselves in positive roles (Guyton, Saxton, and Wesche 1996).

Yet, those minority ethnic teachers who are new to the profession report feeling alienated and say they do not have many opportunities to discuss issues around race and schooling. Few have access to mentoring programs. Instead they create their own support systems by cultivating friendships with other teachers who share similar concerns and ideals. Su (1997) reports, for example, that these teachers find others who want to make a difference in their communities through "establishing a culturally relevant and multiculturally inclusive curriculum" (cited in Quiocho and Rios 2000, 498). Acting as change agents in schools where children are underserved requires leadership skills. By seeking out, organizing, and availing yourself of others' viewpoints and experiences, you too can make opportunities to be in reflexive communities and shape your own teaching practices.

The interactions and relationships that helped these teachers develop their identities as members of specific cultural groups and as professionals (Foster 1994; Galindo 1996; Kanpol 1992; McAlpine and Taylor 1993, cited in Quiocho and Rios 2000) will no doubt help you to do the same. While forming cohorts of teachers who are ready to ask the "difficult questions" may serve to keep you professionally connected, it is important that all teachers in your center or school be brought into the conversation. In order to truly enact multicultural curricula, there must be a "multiplicity of ways people can talk about schooling" (Montecinos 2004, 175). Those who are asking the questions should not be the only ones who seek the answers.

Christina, Part II

Christina knew that one of the most difficult obstacles was going to be her principal who had been in charge for nearly thirty years. Still, she thought she'd take a chance and move the desks yet again, this time staying in rows, but pairing children. This seemed to be a compromise she and her principal could both live with. Only thing was, Christina added a rug to the center of the room where there was a space made by having the desks closer together. When Christina read aloud to the children, she asked them to sit together on the rug. She started the practice of giving out drawing paper and asking the children to make pictures of the part of the story they liked best. She said, "The first time I did this, they all got up and started to go back to their desks. I told them that if they wanted to, they could stay on the rug and work there. I didn't realize how much help they'd need just to loosen up."

The next time I visited, Christina spoke about the room arrangement again. She pointed out the children's work on the walls. One area held their drawings depicting their families. A second area was reserved for "I like me" stories, while yet a third wall held their spelling tests, another compromise Christina made. But, as she said, "All of the children's work is up, regardless of their grade. Each week each kid's work will go right on top of their last week's work. And, I'm about to change from giving them number grades to just having them rewrite the word with the correct spelling and then hanging those up."

Christina had also taken down the stereotypical posters and changed the vocabulary wall to words the children wanted to see go up, words that *they* identified from their reading and told her they wanted up on the wall.

A few months later, as more and more teachers in her school began to "complain" about the noise from Christina's classroom, or the "less disciplined behaviors" of Christina's children, Christina decided to take action. She thought, "You know I've been in this building for six years now and there are some teachers who I've never spoken to. I think if we could just talk and get to know each other, there wouldn't be so much animosity." Christina invited everyone, except the principal, to get together after work. She told everyone there would be "no shop talk" that evening and that it occurred to her that they all needed some time together outside of the school.

When Christina came back to tell me about this, she was elated. "We talked for hours. It was great. There were some people who seemed to be angry at first and wanted to confront me about the changes I made in my classroom, but I didn't let that conversation even get started. We just talked about family, vacation places we'd been. I came in on Monday and felt a whole new atmosphere. The kindergarten teacher keeps coming in my room to ask how I do things and wants me to come to see her room too. This is great."

On my next visit to Christina's second grade classroom, I was astonished at the change I saw in the children. They were animated and freely moved around the room during an observation and recording lesson on mapping. Some children sat on the rug with a pile of markers that, although they belonged to one child, everyone shared. Other children sat in small groups, helping one another attempt to spell words for their narrative descriptions of their drawings. Christina sat with one child who she later told me "needs the attention to concentrate; she's absent so often, it's hard for her to get into the rhythm of things or to catch up." They worked together on a simple map of a zoo, drawn with instructions to find animals and objects. As Christina sat with this child, others came to her to ask questions or make a complaint. Christina mostly responded to them with questions of her own, redirecting their work or implying that they could decide the answer. One change that I noticed was when she asked the children who were having difficulties interacting to step away from their work and figure out the problem, what they'd like to do about it, and then to come and tell her what they decided.

When Christina and I met again, I had been thinking about what she said regarding the way other teachers in her school were viewing the children in her class. I wanted to know how Christina was dealing with this. She said that she did have two teachers who were particularly unkind to her and sometimes chose to take this out on her children, yelling at them in the hall or having them sit out during recess. Christina said that she was handling this by being "polite but firm." She said she had confronted one teacher who she felt had mistreated a child in her class and tried to use DERM to stay focused and clear about what she wanted to get across. She said that although this child had misbehaved, she thought the punishment was excessive and that if this child ever misbehaved again, she would appreciate it if the teacher would send the child to her and she would handle it.

"How did this work out?" I wondered. Christina said that the teacher no longer speaks to her but that she also doesn't interfere with Christina's children. She sends them back to class instead, "which is just fine by me," Christina laughed.

"And the other teacher?"

"Well, I think she feels like she's not the one people go to anymore. She's been teaching for twenty-five years and all the new teachers used to go to her to find out what to do. I did when I first started. But then I realized that she didn't think these kids could learn; that she was just there to get them to memorize stuff and to pass them to the next grade. I stopped going to her when I started going to the community college. I used one of my professors there to get help with any questions I had about teaching. And now, instead of eating my lunch alone in my classroom, there's a group of us who meet at lunchtime and talk about teaching and about kids. She's never come to that group, although anyone is welcome. It's interesting, 'cause we started out just complaining, but then we just kind of started to think about ways to figure things out, and gave each other advice and ideas. Now we visit each other's rooms all the time and I see so many changes, in the teachers and in the children."

- Think about the teachers in your setting. What are some of the traits of the most popular teachers? What are some of the traits of the least popular teachers?
- Think about the teachers in your setting. What are some of the goals for teaching young children that you share? What are some differences? How would you learn from these differences?
- Think about how often you speak with other teachers. How much of your conversations would you consider "teacher talk"? How do these conversations help you with your own practice?
- Have you ever had an opportunity to be a leader for an event? Describe what you did and how you felt.

After Christina graduated I called to congratulate her on a scholarship she had won. Christina told me, "I found my calling. Second grade is my love. Oh, and we're studying animals now . . . and I found out that there's a group in New York City who will bring animals to your classroom! I'm thrilled that I can finally use what I read about hands-on learning. And the parents support me one hundred percent. They see the changes in their kids. There's so much going on and the kids love learning—they ask so many great questions . . . "

Christina has since completed her first year with her second graders. She was offered a leadership position by the Archdiocese. She is on the school's steering committee and continues to mentor the kindergarten teacher. As she said, "Now that I can see what these kids were missing, the whole child approach, I know I'll never go back to that rote way of teaching. You know, helping me see some of the issues in terms of how I was seeing children made me think about the way the school was seeing children. I knew these kids were capable of so much more than we were doing with them. I think there are a lot of teachers in this school who need to be helped to see this too. But I'm not taking the administrative job. I need to stay with second graders for a while, get really good at it, and then I'll think about stepping out of the classroom. Meanwhile, anybody who wants to talk, I'm available."

Beside the amazing changes that I saw in the children in her second grade classroom, Christina's leadership was also outstanding. She was reflective about every aspect of her work, from what the physical space and wall decorations meant to the children, to the ways children used texts, to moving from a "banking approach" to learning to an experiential approach. Christina chose her battles carefully. She stepped out of the way of confrontation but held on to her beliefs and her desire to empower these children with a love for learning. She influenced some of the other teachers and as she said, "The most important thing is that now we all talk to each other.

We may not agree, but at least we're having the conversation and thinking about why we'd choose to do something or not with the kids. I think we've moved into the twenty-first century."

Along these same lines, you may want to develop a collaborative partnership with a co-worker, or a peer in your undergraduate program. In the collaborative learning partnership, you and your partner select one another, share the same goals, and support each other. The benefits come when you both use each other's strengths or expertise to accomplish what you could not have done alone. Often, collaboration focuses on a specific subject or question. The ideas that you each contribute not only enrich the work, they generate more questions and can deepen or challenge the ways you may have been thinking about a particular subject. Offering guiding questions, being able to take risks, learning from mistakes, and being open to feedback should be familiar to you from having been mentored. And, like mentoring, you will need to lay the ground-work and be clear about expectations, including who will do what work. You will need to set goals and talk about the fact that you will take turns being the leader as the work gets done.

Collaboration is often used so that teachers can combine their skills within one classroom, or so that two or more classes can be brought together to work on an extended or integrated curricula. Collaboration is also familiar to early childhood practitioners. We are seldom alone in our classrooms and benefit from having other adults whose personalities, viewpoints, and skills enrich the children's and our own experiences. In collaborating with our classroom team, we not only construct new knowledge, we model working cooperatively, a form of good citizenship, for the children we teach. Modeling cooperative behavior is also good leadership.

Your center or school may also use peer mentoring. This is much like traditional mentoring in that it supports professional and psychosocial development. The differ-ence is that peer mentoring usually happens between teachers who are alike in age, experience, and status. Since this type of mentoring is usually among relatively equal teachers, there may be less formality than in an academic mentorship, and perhaps a greater willingness to discuss issues other than classroom practices.

And, when you have been teaching for a while, think about hosting students in your classroom. Cooperating teachers have reported that some of the benefits to hosting student teachers include opportunities for reflection and reflexivity, having the student bring in new ideas, including academic readings that they are studying in courses, and renewing their appreciation for teamwork (Grisham, Ferguson, and Brink 2004). Other studies report that host teachers felt a greater sense of professionalism, believed they had improved their teaching skills, held a greater status among colleagues, seemed less isolated, and benefited by having more time to attend to individual children since there was another adult in the room (Davies, Brady, Rodger, and Wall 1999, cited in Grisham et al. 2004). Again, considering the idea that there is no teaching without learning, you can see how these cooperating teachers' responses reflect the learning that comes with mentoring others.

My own experience has shown me that although cooperating teachers may have been in classrooms for many years, they still look forward to receiving feedback and talking over ideas. As a host teacher, you can benefit from having the student-teacher's mentor act as a consultant, lending her expertise to your own.

As a potential leader in an early childhood setting, you may find yourself guiding others in your site to consider sharing responsibilities on a rotating basis. For example, different individual staff members or teams could be responsible for organizing and leading staff meetings. This could include developing curriculum ideas, heading a child study, or running a workshop. This shared responsibility gives everyone in the center a sense of ownership. It also gives co-workers time to get to know each other better, to develop trust, and to participate in deeper, more meaningful dialogue. Baldwin (1994, cited in Lipson Lawrence 2002) speaks about this as members of a community "holding the rim" of a circle. All members of the community are responsible for the whole. As a leader, you can help others see that "when commitment is high and contributions from all members are valued, communities have the potential to co-create knowledge, make effective decisions, and effect change" (Lipson Lawrence 2002, 84). And, since this kind of power sharing is not the norm in most centers or schools, you could use what you learned by having been mentored to help others understand the need for open communication, trust, planning, and constructive feedback.

In her excellent chapter on early childhood leadership, "Who's missing at the table? Leadership opportunities and barriers for teachers and providers" (1997), Marcy Whitebook addresses the field's failure to recognize the valuable leadership skills that teachers and early child care/education providers can offer. She makes the point that early childhood classroom teachers often use modes of leadership that may not be valued by the rest of society. Our approaches to educative experiences for young children are not bound to authoritarian rule. We often work alongside children, cooperating and facilitating by asking good questions. We often follow a child's lead and may even find that we may have to step out of the way to know what to do next.

Whitebook also looks at leadership skills that are easily applied to other situations outside the classroom. She points to public policy discussions, where teachers' voices are seldom, if ever, heard. She asserts that although teachers of young children have experiential insights into the needs of children and families, they are seldom allowed to lead the discussion, seldom write for journals, and do not necessarily feel comfortable participating in academic and theoretical debates about issues somewhat removed from their classroom practices.

Whitebook gives an example of how the National Center for the Early Childhood Workforce developed a project in response to requests from local organizations in California to assist and train child care teachers and providers in leadership and advocacy (Leadership Empowerment Action Project [LEAP]). She says of LEAP,

> The training is geared to people at a variety of levels of experience in leadership, organizing, community action, and advocacy—newcomers meeting with other teachers and providers for the first time, budding leaders who have some experience but want to strengthen their skills, and experienced leaders who need help in nurturing new leadership and replenishing themselves. The curriculum is designed around the three critical stages of empowerment: coming to awareness, engaging in inquiry and analysis, and taking action. The training helps teachers and providers articulate their stories, interpret these experiences in the larger context of history and community and use that knowledge to identify appropriate steps toward change. (1997, 80)

Within this larger framework, LEAP offers mentoring to child care providers and teachers. This aspect of the program has helped to build leadership by recognizing and using the skills teachers and providers already have, and by refining and extending these practices. Importantly, Whitebook states that individual programs work to hold onto good teachers by providing financial supports, offering learning opportunities and professional development through peer coaching, reflection, and leadership, while improving the overall quality of early care and education programs. Most importantly, Whitebook affirms that good teachers are good advocates.

Hopefully, by having been in a cooperative, developmentally responsive, critically reflective and reflexive mentoring relationship, you will have learned how to be responsible for and in control of your own learning. Hopefully, with your mentor's help, you will have become empowered to seek out and demand the best from your instructors, your peers, and those who are leaders in your work setting. Hopefully, when you become a mentor, you will have learned to be "(a) critical friend, personal guide, counselor, and fully engaged in a relationship that has the potential to become as fundamental to the personal development of the mentor as to the development of the mentee" (Fletcher 1998, 110). Hopefully, you will also demand the best from the children you teach, and, of course, from yourself.

Teaching and Working for Social Justice

While much of what I have written in this book calls for social justice in adult and teacher education, I would like to focus here on the need to recognize early childhood education as a site in the struggle for social justice. Because of its history, early care/ education continues to be left out of the fiscal frameworks of those who oversee public education. With such a low premium placed on the children who receive this care, the women who provide this care, and the families who need this care, there is much work to be done.

There are many confounding factors that impact the ability of the child care/ education field to meet the needs of the families they serve, including quality, choice, and affordability, attracting and retaining educated caregivers/teachers and directors, paying a worthy wage, and receiving the necessary funding and recognition from local, state, and federal agencies. While there are numerous other statistics that point to the "outsider" status of early childhood educators, one of the most glaring omissions is the fact that there are no national standards or regulations governing who can work with young children. Education levels of teachers who work with young children vary widely. And as one would expect, with this deviation in educational attainments, there is great disparity in pay scales. Besides the most obvious comparisons between nonpublic school preschool teachers' average hourly wages ($9.66) and public school kindergarten teachers' wages ($26.82), there are the wages that other workers receive—bus driver ($13.10) and animal trainer ($12.62)—that allude to the low status of early childhood educators (Bureau of Labor Statistics 2002, cited in Whitebook and Sakai 2004). The differences in wages are even greater when you consider the fact that many early childhood professionals work a full year, and many are without health care benefits, pensions, or union representation.

We know that the quality of classrooms, child outcomes, and effectiveness are directly proportional to the preschool teacher's level of education, specifically related to early childhood (Hamre and Bridges 2004; Tout, Zaslow, and Berry 2005). Yet, with only one third of center-based teachers holding a bachelor's degree or higher (Saluja,

Early, and Clifford 2002), why then do only twenty-five states require pre-service or ongoing education of center-based teachers (Whitebook and Sakai 2004)? What does that say about the way our society thinks about the importance of care and education for its youngest members? What does that say about what others think of the work that early childhood educators do?

Therefore, I suggest that in the case of early childhood care/education, teaching and working for social justice start "at home," in teacher education programs and in child care/education settings. In Finn and Finn's (2007) *Teacher Education with an Attitude,* Rosalie Romano, a professor at Ohio University, addresses just this point:

> Advocacy and action emerge out of awareness, and if there is any hope of a teacher
> moving from social reproduction, due to naiveté, into student advocacy and social
> justice, then consciousness must be raised at the earliest points in a teacher's
> development; in this case, during their licensure program at the preservice level.
> Further, awareness is simply the first stage of recognition of social inequities. The aim
> of awareness should be critical action, action that encourages a particular kind of civic
> courage and that initiates and sustains awareness and action in youth as well. (96)

Teaching and working for social justice "at home" must of course include your relationships with the children and families you serve. These relationships demand that you attend to the more pragmatic obstacles early childhood educators face daily, such as inadequate materials, unbalanced child to adult ratios, co-workers with little or no training, regulation by outside agencies—some of whom demand compliance without discussion—families and children living in stressful situations, ignorance of the community's language and cultures, and others' lack of respect for what you do (Bellm et al. 1997).

As you move through your undergraduate education and into the early childhood profession, I would hope that you are able to find not only a mentor who can help you through the rigors of college, but someone who can provide a model of leadership in the field. In academia, leadership can take the form of having a research agenda that examines current issues in early childhood education: children and families in under-served settings, critical pedagogy in teacher education, women of color as teachers in early childhood settings, men in early childhood education, contextualized adult education, multicultural/multilingual approaches to early care/education, resistance to standardization and high-stakes testing, or equity issues around funding and regulations, to name a few. Most often, the people who are working on these issues are also involved in defining the problems and helping to find solutions. As a mentee and a growing professional, working with your mentor on these issues can offer you different ways of looking at the profession and insight into many other components of the field.

In the practical world of care/education, leadership can come from your director, parents, peers, outside supporters, or governing agencies. When people work together to examine professional practices, the state of the physical environment, regulations that are interconnected or mandates that are in conflict with each other and with what we do, relationships with communities, or funding, they must remember that they are doing all of these things in order to give children safe, nurturing, challenging, and respectful environments.

I raise these issues here to point out that while the early childhood field has moved somewhat toward a professional stance, for example, membership in the

National Association for the Education of Young Children has increased four-fold from 1975 to 1990 (Whitebook 1997), the professional status of the early childhood practitioner has not. Early childhood education is often left out of the general education literature. Although many writers use the generic heading "K-12," the pedagogies discussed are seldom appropriate for the early childhood educator. In New York state, for example, early childhood teacher candidates must take a series of exams before they can be initially certified to teach 0–8-year-olds. This early childhood-specific certification is relatively new, having been the site of struggle by early childhood professionals for many years. This separate certification is considered a necessity by many teacher educators, as we hold that early childhood practices are and should remain distinct. Yet, of the required exams, the state has eliminated the early childhood-specific Content Specialty Exam. Early childhood teacher candidates are required to take the elementary (first through sixth grade) content specialty exam instead, with major essay questions usually based on literacy practices. While early childhood teachers certainly assist young children's language development and emergent literacy, the thrust of the questions and therefore the answers are geared to elementary education practices. As a result, many early childhood majors have difficulty passing this exam, and many universities with early childhood programs read these data as a reflection of the "poor quality" of early childhood teacher candiates rather than the unfairness of the exam's focus.

To confound the issue, there is a movement in New York and other states to yet again change the certification levels to include kindergarten in the elementary certification, and third grade in the early childhood certification. While the fiscal considerations are clear, that public school administrators can hire teachers with wider-ranging certifications, what, I wonder, does this say about the sanctity of the early childhood specialization?

With this approach, and increased reliance on didactic, often scripted "teacher-proof" curricula and testing, how are early childhood practices compromised to meet mandates and increasingly academic expectations of what it means for children to be "ready" for kindergarten or even first grade? Early childhood educators know that the needs, experiences, and pedagogies for these age groups are truly and appropriately different. Early childhood educators must understand this as another site for struggle. In this case, I would suggest that the "push down" of academics and the removal of play from many programs are bullying tactics used by those who are bigger and stronger than we are. I am sure those who hold certifications in other specialized areas would agree—expertise requires concentrated study—or it wouldn't be called a specialty. And being a specialty, why is it that the upper grades aren't learning from our methodologies?

This call for a broader early childhood teacher certification also comes at a time when many state public school systems are offering universal prekindergarten classes, and some are even considering including programs for three-year-olds. While this is a laudable step toward helping young children who might otherwise not be enrolled in child care, Head Start, or nursery school, it is a project that has some questionable practices. For example, there are nowhere near the numbers of well-educated and certified early childhood practitioners needed to teach these young children. Teachers from upper grades who have elementary licenses are being called upon to fill this gap.

Another issue that makes the rush to offer universal pre-K a concern is the fact that most often there are not enough "seats" in public schools to accommodate these children. Many public schools are already enrolled way beyond capacity. The solution in New York, for example, is to "subcontract" universal pre-K programs to child care centers and nursery schools. While I believe this is where universal pre-K programs belong anyhow, there are multiple issues that arise from this arrangement—appropriate teacher mentoring, especially for those trained to teach older children, being one.

While centers and nurseries are given money for materials for the universal pre-K classroom, these monies are provided only for the universal pre-K classroom. I have seen more than one day care center where the pre-K classroom was so full of materials and furniture that children were cramped and overwhelmed. Yet, in the same center, the twos, threes, and kindergarten classrooms were practically bare. Directors of public centers are put in the difficult position of either developing "creative accounting" practices, or not sharing the funds equally among all classrooms. Directors are not being supported as they try to address this inequity, and are often fearful of reprisals if they make decisions outside of the universal pre-K guidelines.

Teachers who have "UPK children" in their classrooms are employees of the child care center or nursery school, yet must follow the state's universal pre-K curriculum and are subject to visits from local departments of education "consultants," many of whom do not hold early childhood certification themselves. Teachers in public day care settings who have universal pre-K children in their classrooms are subject to multiple visits by different "consultants" representing the different governing agencies and bureaucracies that fund their sites. These different consultants can demand different practices, classroom setups, interactions with children, record-keeping systems, levels of parent participation, and they can mandate attendance at different meetings. Each agency and each consultant expects compliance and naturally sees his or her own set of regulations as paramount. What's a teacher to do? In these instances, the teacher/consultant relationship is hardly a mentoring relationship, as most teachers with whom I have spoken see it as evaluative and not professional development. Ramon, the teacher whose story you read in Chapter 1, offers just one solution.

These somewhat stilted relationships are also fraught with resentment since day care teachers do not receive the same overall compensation as public school teachers, yet they are teaching the same children with the same curriculum. Many of the universal pre-K programs are only funded for part of the school day. While there may be a pay differential for the hours a day that the day care or nursery class must enact the universal pre-K curriculum, often 9:00 A.M. to 11:30 A.M., the children remain the same children throughout the day, sometimes arriving at 8:00 A.M. and staying until 6:00 P.M. The work remains the same as well, although I have heard teachers differentiate children by labeling some "UPK kids" and others "day care kids." How this affects teacher/child relationships is an important subject for future study.

Perhaps if you find yourself in this situation and have had a positive mentoring experience, you too can assertively request that an evaluative association evolve into a supervisory relationship.

Teaching and learning for equity and social justice begins "at home." The mentoring relationship can become a place for you to try on ideas not only about early childhood practices, but about the kind of school or center in which you would like to work.

By taking a broader view of care/education of the young child, you can begin to question your role as it has been historically defined by others. In the safety of the mentoring relationship, you can begin to remake child care/education settings according to your vision.

For many children and even for some adults, schools are not friendly places. By seeking out and developing a mentoring relationship where you can speak about some of these topics, you may be able to break the cycle of underserved and prescribed schooling that you may encounter in the field. You will also be in a better position to demand an education that meets your own needs and insist that you be an active participant in your own learning. Once you are adept at this, you will be able to offer these same approaches to learning to the young children in your classrooms. You will be working for social justice and equity at the grassroots level and on a daily basis.

And it is imperative that the cycle of poor education for poor children be broken. For those of you who will work in public schools or nursery settings, you will have the benefit of being perceived as working in an educational environment, but for those of you who will teach in day care or Head Start, you will most likely struggle to help others see what you do as educative. While caring for children is part of educating children, you will need to actively and continually teach those outside the profession about your work.

The quality of care and education, and therefore more positive outcomes for young children, are significantly affected by the level of teacher qualifications (McMullen and Alat 2002). Teachers with four-year degrees not only more often provide high-quality classroom experiences, they bring a "depth and breadth of education and experience, exposure to the world of ideas and perspectives, along with the skills to communicate and express their knowledge fluidly . . ." (McMullen and Alat 2002, conclusion). Bringing this educated stance to early childhood classrooms not only enhances your approaches to culturally relevant teaching, it supports your commitment to the profession, and most importantly to the academic and personal success of the young children in your care.

I mention all of the above to call attention to the need for the creation of new mentoring networks in the field of early childhood education. As large cohorts of experienced teachers and mentors retire from the field, there will be numerous opportunities for newer practitioners to redefine the work of the mentor. As Andy Hargreaves and Michael Fullan advise, mentors should not be "tormentors" but instead the mentoring relationship must become "less hierarchical, less individualistic, more wide-ranging, and more inclusive in its orientation than it has been viewed in the past" (2000, 54). Mentoring must evolve to meet the needs of the twenty-first-century teacher.

Being mentored should become the norm rather than the exception. Being mentored should be built into teacher education, preparing you to enact change and redefine teaching for yourself, as well as for the children you teach. Being mentored must become an integral part of your daily life in schools and child care centers. Being mentored ought to support your vision of yourself as a professional, so that when you are ready to mentor others, you will see yourself as imparting professional knowledge and being accountable to other members of the teaching community.

Being mentored has the potential to become a force for change in the teaching profession. By using critical reflection, participating in reflexive exchange, enacting supervision instead of evaluation, constructing knowledge of learning styles and cultural influences, and sharing definitions of learning and teaching, you, as part of the mentoring team, will have already changed the face of traditional mentoring. And it is my guess that if you experience this kind of mentoring relationship, being a teacher will not only be the work you do with children and families, but will be a way for you to experience ongoing, lifelong learning as well.

References

Acheson, K. A., & Gall, M. D. (1997). *Techniques in the clinical supervision of teachers: Preservice and inservice applications* (4th ed). New York: Wiley & Sons.

Allen, T. D., & Eby, L. T. (2004). Factors related to mentor reports of mentoring provided: Gender and relational characteristics. *Sex Roles, 50*(1/2), 129–139.

Aslanian, C. (1996). *Adult learning in America: Why and how adults go back to school.* New York: The College Board.

Ayers, W. (Ed.). (1995). *To become a teacher: Making a difference in children's lives.* New York: Teachers College Press.

Baldwin, C. (1994). *Calling the circle.* Newburg, OR: Swan Raven.

Bauman, S. S-M., Wang, N., DeLeon, C. W., Kafentzis, J., Zavala-Lopez, M., & Lindsey, M. S. (2004). Non-traditional students' service needs and social support resources: A pilot study. *Journal of College Counseling. 7,* 13–17.

Belenky, M. F., Clinchy, B. M., Goldberger, N. R., & Tarule, J. M. (1997). *Women's ways of knowing: The development of self, voice and mind.* New York: Basic Books.

Bell, C. R. (2000). The mentor as partner. *Training & Development, 54*(2) 53–56.

Bellm, D., Whitebook, M., & Hnatiuk, P. (1997). *The early childhood mentoring curriculum: A handbook for mentors.* Washington, D C: Center for the Childcare Workforce.

Benishek, L. A., Bieschke, K. J., Park, J., & Slattery, S. (2004). A multicultural feminist model of mentoring. *Journal of Multicultural Counseling and Development, 32,* 428–442.

Bey, T. M., & Holmes, C. T. (Eds.). (1990). *Mentoring: Contemporary principles and issues.* Reston, VA: Association of Teacher Educators.

Biesta, G. J. J., & Burbules, N. C. (2003). *Pragmatism and educational research.* Lanham, MD: Rowman & Littlefield.

Bourdieu, P., & Waquant, L. (1992). *An invitation to reflexive sociology.* Chicago: University of Chicago Press.

Bowman, S. R., Kite, M. E., Branscombe, N. R., & Williams, S. (2000). Developmental relationships of black Americans in the academy. In A. J. Murrell, F. J. Crosby, & R. J. Ely (Eds.), *Mentoring dilemmas: Developmental relationships within multicultural organizations.* Mahwah, NJ: Erlbaum.

Bredekamp, S., & Copple, C. (1997). *Developmentally appropriate practice in early childhood programs.* Washington, DC: National Association for the Education of Young Children.

Britzman, D., Dippo, D., Searle, D., & Pitt, A. (1997). Toward an academic framework for thinking about teacher education. *Teaching Education, 9,* 15–26.

Brookfield, S. (1986). *Understanding and facilitating adult learning: A comprehensive analysis of principles and effective practices.* San Francisco: Jossey-Bass.

Brookfield, S. D. (1995). *Becoming a critically reflective teacher.* San Francisco: Jossey-Bass.

Brown, S. (2003). Working models: Why mentoring programs may be the key to teacher retention. *Techniques (Association for Career and Technical Education),* *78*(5), 18–21.

Bunting, C. (1988). Cooperating teachers and the changing views of teacher candidates. *Journal of Teacher Education, 39*(2), 42–46.

Bureau of Labor Statistics. (2002). Labor Force Participation Rates, 2001–2010, Labor Force (Demographic) Data, Employment Projections. Washington, DC: Office of Occupational Statistics and Employment Projections, Bureau of Labor Statistics, U.S. Department of Labor. Available at ftp://ftp.bls.gov/pub/specialrequests/ep/labor.force/clra0110.txt

Burk Rodgers, D., & Dunn, M. (2000). Sara's internship experience: Relationships and autonomy. *Action in Teacher Education, 22*(3), 19–29.

Campbell, D., & Campbell, T. A. (2000). The mentoring relationship: Differing perceptions of benefits. *College Student Journal, 34*(4), 516–523.

Carney-Crompton, S., & Tan, J. (2002). Support systems, psychological functioning, and academic performance of nontraditional female students. *Adult Education Quarterly, 52*(2), 140–154.

Carter, M., & Curtis, D. (1994). *Training teachers: A harvest of theory and practice.* St. Paul, MN: Redleaf Press.

Clark, E., Riojas, F., & Bustos, B. (2002). Narrowing the pipeline for ethnic minority teachers: Standards and high-stakes testing. *Multicultural Perspectives, 4*(2), 15–20.

Cohen, N. H. (1995). *Mentoring adult learners: A guide for educators and trainers.* Melbourne, FL: Krieger.

Credle, J. O., & Dean, G. J. (1991). A comprehensive model for enhancing black student retention in higher education. *Journal of Multicultural Counseling and Development, 19,* 158–165.

Cropper, A. (2000). Mentoring as an inclusive device for the excluded: Black students' experience of a mentoring scheme. *Social Work Education, 19*(6), 597–606.

Daloz, L. A. (1999). *Mentor: Guiding the journey of adult learners.* San Francisco: Jossey-Bass.

Davies, M. A., Brady, M., Rodger, E., & Wall, P. (1999). Mentors and school-based partnership: Ingredients for professional growth. *Action in Teacher Education, 21*(1), 85–96.

Deci, E. L., Eghrari, H., Patrick, B. C., & Leone, D. R. (1994). Facilitating internalization: The self-determination theory perspective. *Journal of Personality, 62*(1), 119–142.

Delpit, L. (1986). *Other people's children: Cultural conflict in the classroom.* The New Press: New York.

Dewey, J. (1916/1958). *Experience and education.* New York: McMillan.

Dewey, J. (1933). *How we think.* Chicago: Regnery.

Duckworth, E. R. (2006). *The having of wonderful ideas and other essays on teaching and learning* (3rd ed.). New York: Teachers College Press.

Edwards, R., Ranson, S., & Strain, M. (2002). Reflexivity: Towards a theory of lifelong learning. *International Journal of Lifelong Education, 21*(6), 525–536.

Eppler, M. A., & Harju, B. L. (1997). Achievement motivation goals in relation to academic performance in traditional and nontraditional college students. *Research in Higher Education, 38*(5), 557–573.

Fassinger, R. E. (1997). *Dangerous liaisons: Reflections on feminist mentoring.* Invited "Woman of the Year" Award address presented at the annual meeting of the American Psychology Association, Chicago, IL.

Feist-Price, S. (1994). Cross-gender mentoring relationships: Critical issues. *Journal of Rehabilitation,* 13–17.

Finn, P. J., & Finn M. E. (Eds.). (2007). *Teacher education with an attitude: Preparing teachers to educate working-class students in their collective self-interest.* Albany, NY: State University of New York Press.

Fletcher, S. (1998). Attaining self-actualization through mentoring. *European Journal of Teacher Education, 21*(1), 109–118.

Foley, G. (2005). Educational institutions: Supporting working-class learning. *New Directions for Adult & Continuing Education, 106,* 37–44.

Foster, M. (1994). The role of community and culture in school reform efforts: Examining the views of African-American teachers. *Educational Foundations, 8*(2), 5–26.

Fox, W., & Gay. G. (1995). Integrating multicultural and curriculum principles in teacher education. *Peabody Journal of Education, 70,* 64–82.

Freeman, K. (1999). No services needed? The case for mentoring high-achieving African American students. *Peabody Journal of Education, 74*(2), 15–26.

Freire, P. (1970). *Pedagogy of the oppressed.* New York: Continuum Publishing.

Freire, P. (2005). *Teachers as cultural workers: Letters to those who dare teach.* Cambridge, MA: Westview Press.

Galbraith, M. W. (Ed.). (1991). *Facilitating adult learning: A transactional process.* Malabar, FL: Krieger.

Galindo, R. (1996). Reframing the past in the present: Chicana teacher role identity as a bridging identity. *Education and Urban Society, 29,* 85–102.

Gardner, H. (1983). *Frames of mind: The theory of multiple intelligences.* New York: Basic Books.

Goldhammer, R. (1969). *Clinical supervision.* New York: Holt, Rinehart and Winston.

Gonzalez Meña, J. (2005). *Diversity in early care and education: Honoring differences* (4th ed.). New York: McGraw-Hill.

Gonzalez Rodriguez, Y. E., & Sjostrom, B. R. (1998). Critical reflection for professional development: A comparative study of nontraditional adult and traditional student teachers. *Journal of Teacher Education, 4*(3), 177–186.

Graham, P. (1997). Tensions in the mentor teacher-student teacher relationship: Creating productive sites for learning within a high school English teacher education program. *Teacher and Teacher Education, 13*(5), 513–527.

Graham, D., & Donaldson, J. F. (1999). Adult students' academic and intellectual development in college. *Adult Education Quarterly, 49*(3), 147–162.

Granados, R., & Lopez, J. M. (1999). Student-run support organizations for underrepresented graduate students: Goals, creation, implementation, and assessment. *Peabody Journal of Education, 74*(2), 135–149.

Gray, W. A., & Gray, M. M. (1985). Synthesis of research on mentoring beginning teachers. *Educational Leadership, 43*(3), 37–43.

Gregory, S., & Sanjek, R. (1994). *Race.* New Brunswick, NJ: Rutgers University Press.

Griggs, S., & Dunn, R. (1995). Hispanic-American students and learning style. *Emergency Librarian, 23*(2), 11–17.

Grisham, D. L., Ferguson, J. L., & Brink, B. (2004). Mentoring the mentors: Student teacher contributions to the middle school classroom. *Mentoring and Tutoring, 12*(3), 307–319.

Guy, T. (1999). Culture as context for adult education: The need for culturally relevant adult education. *New Directions for Adult and Continuing Education, 82,* 5–18.

Guyton, E., Saxton, R., & Wesche, M. (1996). Experiences of diverse students in teacher education. *Teaching & Teacher Education, 12*(6), 643–652.

Hamilton, K. (2002). Race in the college classroom. *Black Issues in Higher Education, 19*(2), 32–36.

Hamre, B. K., & Bridges, M. (2004). Early care and education staff preparation, quality, and child development: A review of the literature. Manuscript submitted for publication.

Hansman, C. A. (1998). Mentoring and women's career development. *New Directions for Adult and Continuing Education, 80,* 63–70.

Hargreaves, A., & Fullan, M. (2000). Mentoring in the new millennium. *Theory into Practice, 39*(1), 50–56.

Haring, M. J. (1999). The case for a conceptual base for minority mentoring programs. *Peabody Journal of Education, 74*(2), 5–14.

Haring, M. J., & Freeman, K. (1999). Editor's introduction. *Peabody Journal of Education. 74*(2), 1–4.

Heinrich, K. T. (1995). Doctoral advisement relationships between women: On friendship and betrayal. *Journal of Higher Education, 66*(4), 447–469.

Herman, L., & Mandell, A. (2004). *From teaching to mentoring: Principle and practice, dialogue and life in adult Education.* London: RoutledgeFalmer.

Heung-Ling, Y. (2003). Mentor student-teacher case studies. *Early Child Development and Care, 173*(1), 33–41.

Hoffman-Kipp, P., Artiles, A. J., & Lopez-Torres, L. (2003). Beyond reflection: Teacher learning as praxis. *Theory into Practice, 42*(3), 248–254.

Hollingsworth, S. (1989). Prior beliefs and cognitive change in learning to teach. *American Educational Research Journal, 26*(2), 160–189.

Home, A. (1998). Predicting role conflict, overload and contagion in adult women university students with families and jobs. *Adult Education Quarterly, 48,* 85–98.

House, J. S. (1981). *Work stress and social support.* Reading, MA: Addison-Wesley.

Houser, M. L. (2005). Are we violating their expectations? Instructor communication expectations of traditional and nontraditional students. *Communication Quarterly, 53*(2), 213–228.

Howes, C., James, J., & Ritchie, S. (2003). Pathways to effective teaching. *Early Childhood Research Quarterly, 18*(1), 104–120.

Hyun, E., & Marshall, J. D. (1997). Theory of multiple/multiethnic perspective-taking ability for teachers' developmentally and culturally appropriate practice (DCAP). *Journal of Research in Childhood Education, 11,* 188–198.

Irvine, J. J. (1989). Beyond role models: An examination of cultural influences on the pedagogical practices of black teachers. *Peabody Journal of Education, 66,* 51–63.

Jacobi, M. (1991). Mentoring and undergraduate academic success: A literature review. *Review of Educational Research, 61,* 505–532.

Jaramillo, J. A. (1996). Vygotsky's sociocultural theory and contributions to the development of constructivist curricula. *Education, 117,* 133–140.

Jenks, C., Lee, J. O., & Kanpol, B. (2001). Approaches to multicultural education in preservice teacher education: Philosophical frameworks and models for teaching. *The Urban Review, 3*(2), 87–105.

Jipson, J. A., & Munro, P. (1997). Deconstructing wo/mentoring: Diving into the abyss. In J. Jipson & N. Paley (Eds.), *Daredevil research: Re-creating analytical practice* (pp. 201–217). New York: Teachers College Press.

Johnson, S., & Robson, C. (1999). Threatened identities: The experiences of women in transition to programs of professional higher education. *Journal of Community and Applied Social Psychology, 9,* 273–288.

Johnson, W. B., & Huwe, J. M. (2003). *Getting mentored in graduate school.* Washington, DC: American Psychological Association.

Johnson-Bailey, J. (2002). Race matters: The unspoken variable in the teaching-learning transaction. *New Directions in Adult and Continuing Education, 93,* 39–49.

Johnson-Bailey, J., & Cervero, R. (1997). *Beyond facilitation in adult education: Power dynamics in teaching and learning practices.* Paper presented at the 27th Annual SCUTREA Crossing borders, breaking boundaries: Research in the Education of Adults Conference. Retrieved October 26, 2006, from http://www.leeds.ac.uk/educol/.

Johnson-Bailey, J., & Cervero, R. (2002). Cross-cultural mentoring as a context for learning. *New Directions in Adult and Continuing Education, 86,* 15–26.

Kagan, S. L., & Bowman, B. T. (1997). *Leadership in early care and education.* Washington, DC: National Association for Education of Young Children.

Kanpol, B. (1992). The politics of similarity within difference: A pedagogy for the other. *Urban Review, 24,* 105–131.

Kanpol, B. (1998). *Critical pedagogy for beginning teachers: The movement from despair to hope.* Retrieved August 23, 2006, from http://www.lib.umwestern.edu/pub/jcp/issueII-1/kanpol.html

Kanpol, B. (1999). *Critical pedagogy: An introduction.* Westport, CT: Bergin & Garvey.

Kappner, A. S., & Lieberman, A. (2002). *Joining forces: The role of higher education in preparing the early childhood workforce.* Paper delivered at A Joint Founders' Symposium of the Carnegie Foundation, June 24, 2002, New York.

Katz, L. (1972). Developmental stages of pre-school teachers. *The Elementary School Journal, 23,* 50–51.

Kay, B., & Jacobson, B. (1996). Reframing mentoring. *Training and Development, 5*(8), 44–47. (ERIC Document Reproduction Service No. EJ 548 533)

Kegan, R. (2000). What 'form' transforms? A constructive-developmental approach to transformative learning. In J. Mezirow (Ed.), *Learning as transformation: Critical perspectives on a theory in progress* (pp. 35–69). San Francisco: Jossey-Bass.

Kelly, E. W., Jr. (1997). Relationship-centered counseling: A humanistic model of integration. *Journal of Counseling & Development, 75,* 337–345.

Kenway, J., & McLeod, J. (2004). Bourdieu's reflexive sociology and "spaces of points of view": Whose reflexivity, which perspective? *British Journal of Sociology of Education, 25*(4), 525–544.

Kerka, S. (1998). *New perspectives on mentoring.* (ERIC Digest 194). ERIC Clearinghouse on Adult Career and Vocational Education. Columbus, OH. (ERIC Document Reproduction Service No ED 418 249)

Kerka, S. (2000). *Multiple intelligences and adult education.* (Trends and Issues Alert No. 17.) ERIC Clearinghouse on Adult Career and Vocational Education. Columbus, OH. (ERIC Document Reproduction Service No. ED 446 233)

Kerka, S. (2001). *The balancing act of adult life.* ERIC Clearinghouse on Adult Career and Vocational Education. Columbus, OH.

(ERIC Document Reproduction Service No. ED 459 323)

Knowles, M. (1990). *The adult learner: A neglected species.* (4th ed.). Houston, TX: Gulf.

Kochan, F. K. (2002). Examining the organizational and human dimensions of mentoring: A textual data analysis. In F. K. Kochan (Ed.), *The organizational and human dimensions of successful mentoring programs and relationships* (pp. 269–286). Greenwich, CT: Information Age.

Kochan, F. K., & Pascarelli, J. T. (2003). Mentoring as transformation: Initiating the dialogue. In F. K. Kochan & J. T. Pascarelli, *Global perspectives on mentoring: Transforming contexts, communities, and cultures* (pp. ix–xvii). Greenwich, CT: Information Age.

Kozol, J. (1991). *Savage inequalities.* New York: Crown.

Kram, K. E. (1985). *Mentoring at work.* Glenview, IL: Scott, Forsman and Co.

Lange, E. A. (2004). Transformative and restorative learning: A vital dialectic for sustainable societies. *Adult Education Quarterly, 54*(2), 121–139.

Langer, A. M. (2001). Confronting theory: The practice of mentoring non-traditional students at Empire State College. *Mentoring & Tutoring, 9*(1), 49–62.

Lee, S., Theoharis, R., Fitzpatrick, M., Kim, K., Liss, J. M., Nix-Williams, T., Griswold, D. E., & Walther-Thomas, C. (2006). Create effective mentoring relationships: Strategies for mentor and mentee success. *Intervention in School and Clinic, 41,* 233–240.

Lipson Lawrence, R. (2002). A small circle of friends: Cohort groups as learning communities. *New Directions for Adult and Continuing Education, 95,* 83–92.

Mancuso-Edwards, F. (1993). Behind the door: Disadvantaged students. In A. Levine (Ed.), *Higher learning in America: 1980–2000* (pp. 309–321). Baltimore, MD: The Johns Hopkins University Press.

Manglitz, E., Johnson-Bailey, J., & Cervero, R. M. (2005). Struggles of hope: How white adult educators challenge racism.

Teachers College Record, 107(6), 1245–1274.

Martin, A., & Trueax, J. (1997). Transformative dimensions of mentoring: Implications for practice in the training of early childhood teachers. In *China-U.S. Conference on Education. Collected Papers.* Beijing, People's Republic of China, July 9–13, 1997. (ERIC Document Reproduction Service No. ED 425 405)

McAlpine, A., & Taylor, D. M. (1993). Instructional preferences of Cree, Inuit, and Mohawk teachers. *Journal of American Indian Education, 33,* 1–20.

McAuley, M. J. (2003). Transference, countertransference and mentoring: The ghost in the process. *British Journal of Guidance & Counselling, 31*(1), 11–23.

McCormick, T. (1997). An analysis of five pitfalls of traditional mentoring for people on the margins in higher education. In H. T. Frierson, Jr. (Ed.), *Diversity in higher education* (Vol. 1, pp. 187–202). Greenwich, CT: JAI.

McMullen, M. B., & Alat, K. (2002). Education matters in the nurturing of the beliefs of preschool caregivers and teachers. *Early Childhood Research and Practice, 4*(2). Retrieved January. 28, 2004, from http://ecrp.uiuc.edu/v4n2/mcmullen.html

Mezirow, J., and Associates. (1990). *Fostering critical reflection in adulthood: A guide to transformative and emancipatory learning.* San Francisco: Jossey-Bass.

Mezirow, J. (1991). *Transformative dimensions of adult learning.* San Francisco: Jossey-Bass.

Mezirow, J. (1996). Contemporary paradigms of learning. *Adult Education Quarterly, 46,*158–173.

Mezirow, J. (1997). Transformative learning: Theory to practice. *New Directions for Adult and Continuing Education, 74,* 5–12.

Montecinos, C. (2004). Paradoxes in multicultural teacher education research: Students of color positioned as objects while ignored as subjects. *International Journal of Qualitative Studies in Education, 17*(2), 167–181.

Mullen, C. A., Cox, M. D., Boettcher, C. K., & Adoue, D. S. (2000). *Breaking the circle of one: Redefining mentorship in the lives and writings of educators* (2nd ed.). New York: Peter Lang.

Mullen, C. A., Whatley, A., & Kealy, W. A. (2000). Widening the circle: Faculty-student support groups as innovative practice in higher education. *Interchange: A Quarterly Review of Education, 31*(1), 35–60.

Murrell, A. J., Crosby, J., & Ely, R. J. (Eds.). (1999). *Mentoring dilemmas: Developmental relationships within multicultural organizations.* Mahwah, NJ: Lawrence Erlbaum.

Norman, D. M., & Ganser, T. (2004). A humanistic approach to new teacher mentoring: A counseling perspective. *Journal of Humanistic Counseling, Education and Development 43*(Fall), 129–140.

Ortiz-Walters, R., & Gilson, L. L. (2005). Mentoring in academia: An examination of the experiences of protégés of color. *Journal of Vocational Behavior, 67,* 459–475.

Owen, C., & Soloman, L. Z. (2006). The importance of interpersonal similarities in the teacher mentor/protégé relationship. *Social Psychology of Education, 9,* 83–89.

Perry, W. G. (1999). *Forms of ethical intellectual development in the college years: A scheme.* San Francisco: Jossey-Bass.

Quiocho, A., & Rios, F. (2000). The power of their presence: Minority group teachers and schooling. *Review of Educational Research, 70*(4), 485–528.

Recruiting New Teachers (RNT). (2000). *Teaching the next generation: A national study of precollegiate teacher recruitment.* Belmont, MA. Retrieved April 23, 2001, from www.rnt.org

Rintell, E. M., & Pierce, M. (2003). Becoming maestra: Latina paraprofessionals as teacher candidates in bilingual education. *Journal of Hispanic Higher Education, 2*(1), 5–14.

Rogers, C. (1965). *Client-centered therapy, its current practice, implications, and theory.* Boston: Houghton Mifflin.

Romano, R. M. (2007). Learning to act: Interactive performance and preservice teacher education. In P. Finn & M. Finn (Eds.), *Teacher education with an attitude: Preparing teachers to educate working-class students in their collective self-interest* (pp. 95–110). Albany, NY: State University of New York Press.

Saluja, G., Early, D., & Clifford, R. M. (2002). Demographic characteristics of early childhood teachers and structural elements of early care and education in the United States. *Early Childhood Research and Practice, 4*(1). Retrieved July 12, 2006, from http://ecrp.uiuc.edu/4vn1/saluja.html

Sawchuk, P. H. (2003). *Adult learning and technology in working-class life.* New York: Cambridge University Press.

Schön, D. (1983). *The reflective practitioner: How professionals think in action.* New York: Basic Books.

Scisney-Matlock, M., & Matlock, J. (2001). Promoting understanding of diversity through mentoring undergraduate students. *New Directions for Teaching and Learning, 85,* 75–84.

Shearer, C. B. (1998). *The MIDAS for adults.* Columbus, OH: Greydon Press.

Seigfried, C. H. (2001). John Dewey's pragmatist feminism. In C. H. Seigfried (Ed.), *Feminist interpretations of John Dewey* (pp. 47–77). PA: Pennstate Press.

Sleeter, C. E. (1996). *Multicultural education as social activism.* Albany, NY: State University of New York Press.

Stake, R. E. (1967). The countenance of educational evaluation. *Teachers College Record, 68,* 523–540.

Strage, A. (2008). Traditional and non-traditional college students' descriptions of the "ideal" professor and the "ideal" course and perceived strengths and limitations. *College Student Journal 42*(1), 225–231.

Su, Z. (1997). Teaching as a profession and as a career: Minority candidates' perspectives. *Teaching & Teacher Education, 13,* 325–340.

Tisdell, E. J. (1998). Poststructural feminist pedagogies: The possibilities and limitations of feminist emancipatory adult learning theory and practice. *Adult Education Quarterly, 48*(3), 139–156.

Tout, K., Zaslow, M., & Berry, D. (2005). Quality and qualifications: Links between professional development and quality in early care and education settings. In M. Zaslow & I. Martinez-Beck (Eds.), *Critical issues in early childhood professional development* (pp. 77–110). Baltimore: Brookes Publishing.

Trubowitz, S., & Robbins, M. P. (2003). *The good teacher mentor: Setting the standard for support and success.* New York: Teachers College Press.

Vander Ven, K. (1988). Pathways for professional effectiveness for early childhood educators. In B. Spodek, O. N. Saracho, & D. L. Peters (Eds.), *Professionalism and the early childhood practitioner* (pp. 137–160). New York: Teachers College Press.

Vasquez, V. M. (2004). *Negotiating critical literacies with young children.* Mahwah, NJ: Erlbaum.

Vermunt, J. D., & Vermetten, Y. J. (2004). Patterns in student learning: Relationships between learning strategies, conceptions of learning, and learning orientations. *Educational Psychology Review 16*(4), 359–384.

Vygotsky, L. (1978). *Mind in society: The development of higher psychological processes.* Cambridge, MA: Harvard University Press.

Vygotsky, L. (1986). *Thought and language* (A. Kozulin, Ed. and Trans.). Cambridge, MA: The MIT Press.

Walkerdine, V., Lucey, H., & Melody, J. (2001). *Growing up girl: Psychosocial explorations of gender and class.* New York: New York University Press.

Werring, C. J. (1987). Responding to the older aged full-time student: Preferences for undergraduate education. *College Student Affairs Journal, 1,* 13–20.

Whitebook, M. (1997). Who's missing at the table? Leadership opportunities and barriers for teachers and providers. In S. L. Kagan & B. T. Bowman (Eds.), *Leadership in early care and education* (pp. 77–84). Washington, DC: National Association for Education of Young Children.

Whitebook, M., & Sakai, L. (2004). *By a thread. How child care centers hold on to teachers, how teachers build lasting careers.* Kalamazoo, MI: W. E. Upjohn Institute for Employment Research.

Winant, H. (1994). *Racial conditions: Politics, theory, comparisons.* Minneapolis: University of Minnesota Press.

Yarborough, D. (2002). The engagement model for effective academic advising with undergraduate college students and student organizations. *Journal of Humanistic Counseling Education and Development, 41,* 61–68.

Yopp, R. H., Yopp, H. K., & Taylor, H. P. (1992). Profiles and viewpoints of minority candidates in a teacher diversity project. *Teacher Education Quarterly, 19*(3), 29–48.

Name Index

Subject Index

A

Academic advisors, 30, 31b, 32
Access to education, 34–36
Access within the academy, 34
Adult learners
  age differences with their mentors, 86
  andragogical model of, 7–8
  defined, 7
  "immaturity of," 10
  mentoring others, 90
  motivation in, 77
  nontraditional undergraduates, 6–7
  optimal conditions for, 9
  reflection by, 12–13
Advisors, academic, 30, 31b, 32
Age differences in mentoring relationships, 85–87
Ambivalent learning orientation, 72t, 73
Andragogical model of learning, 7–8, 10–11
Appraisal support, 66
Assertiveness, 67

B

"Banking model" of schooling, 8–9
Business world, mentoring in, 84, 85

C

Certificate learning orientation, 72t, 73
Certification, early childhood, 98
Child(ren)
  in humanistic approach to early childhood
    classrooms, 14, 15, 16
  reasons for teaching and, 89
  validating feelings of, 15
Classroom setup, 62, 91–92
Client-centered therapy, 15
Clinical supervision
  feedback conference phase of, 56–58
  observation phase of, 56
  planning conference phase of, 55–56
  questions to consider before being observed, 55b
  student case-study on, 58–61
Collaboration, 53, 91, 94
Colleagues, being mentored by, 63–64
College catalogue, 33–34
College faculty. See faculty, college
Colleges and universities
  advisement from faculty in, 41
  culture of power in, 35–36
  mentored by professors in, 48–50

organizing educational goals for, 30–31
researching courses in, 31–32
rules within, 33–34
Concepts of learning, 72t, 73
Concrete processing, 72t, 73
Consultants, education, 64–65, 99
Content Specialty Exam, 98
Cooperating teachers
  benefits of hosting student teachers, 94
  match with student teacher, 80–81
  protocols for working with, 52–54
  relationship with, 50–51
Cooperative learning, 73
Courses, college, 31–32
Critical pedagogy, 26
Critical processing, 71, 73
Critical reflection, 21–23, 82, 89
Critical theory, 21
Critical transformative learning, 77
Cross-cultural mentoring relationship, 82–83
Cross-ethnicity mentoring relationships, 78–79
Cross-gender mentoring relationships, 78–79, 83–85
Culture, learning styles and, 11, 69–70, 71b
"Culture of power," 35–36

D

Day care teachers, 99
Deep processing, 71, 72t
Dependence, 10
D.E.R.M. technique, 67–68
Dialogue, in mentoring relationship, 12
Directors, 61–63
Diversity, student, 4–11. *see also* ethnic/racial minorities

E

Early childhood education
  fieldwork required by programs for, 1, 2
  humanistic approach to mentoring and, 14–15
  leadership opportunities in, 95–96
  new mentoring networks in, 100
  opportunities to reflect in, 88
  reasons for wanting to teach in, 89
  shared communication in, 11–12
  struggle for social justice in, 96–101
  written plans and, 56
Early Childhood Mentoring Curriculum, The (Bellm/
    Whitebook/Hnatiuk), 17–18
Early childhood-specific certification, 98
Education consultants, 64–65, 99